M000168750

THE FOUR FRIENDSHIPS
FROM ARISTOTLE TO AQUINAS

Kevin Vost

THE FOUR
FRIENDSHIPS

From Aristotle to Aquinas

✝

Foreword by
SHANE KAPLER

❁ Angelico Press

First published in the USA by Angelico Press
© Kevin Vost 2018
Foreword © Shane Kapler 2018

For information, address:
Angelico Press
169 Monitor St.
Brooklyn, NY 11222
angelicopress.com

ISBN 978-1-62138-325-3 (pbk)
ISBN 978-1-62138-324-6 (cloth)
ISBN 978-1-62138-326-0 (eBook)

✝

Cover design: Michael Schrauzer

CONTENTS

Dedication

To Kathy Ann Vost, my better half and second self,
to Shane Kapler, a truly virtuous spiritual friend,

to Diane Lacopo, once literal neighbor,
always cherished friend

Foreword

I WOULD WAGER that the majority of this book's readers are already familiar with Kevin Vost through his numerous books and media appearances. He is the quintessential Catholic renaissance man—galvanizing the thought of St. Thomas Aquinas and the Dominicans, Aristotle and the Stoics to equip the man and woman in the pew to seek holiness in body and soul. Yes, like you, I know this Kevin Vost and am grateful for the work God has accomplished through him.

Over the past eight years, however, I have also enjoyed the tremendous blessing of knowing the private man. He *is* a brilliant scholar; but he is also a husband, father, mentor, beer aficionado, and friend. I have seen him in action in each of those roles and have been a beneficiary of the final three—but especially the last. I am constantly amazed by Kevin's magnanimity, the way he quietly works to help me and everyone else around him to develop their talents and succeed in whatever undertakings the Lord has assigned. He is the type of friend that each of us aspires to be.

Within the pages that follow, Kevin draws back the curtain to reveal the science of friendship to which Christ introduced him. We encounter the piercing reason of Aristotle and Cicero and the powerful, faith-filled minds of St. Aelred and St. Thomas. It is a feast to be sure. By all means, though, pace yourself; this food is rich!

Perhaps you have heard the expression, "Those who can, *do.* Those who do it best, *teach others.*" Let me assure you, from years of personal experience, that in Kevin Vost you have a master teacher.

SHANE KAPLER
January 28, 2017
Memorial of St. Thomas Aquinas

Preface:
How This Book Came to Be

But when I read the many passages on friendship in the writings of the holy fathers, wishing to love spiritually but not able to, I decided to write on spiritual friendship and to set down for myself rules for a pure and holy love.

⁓ St. Aelred of Rievaulx,
Spiritual Friendship, Prologue[1]

By JANUARY of 2009 I had been familiar with the writings of Aristotle and Cicero for decades, with those of St. Thomas Aquinas for about five years, and was just about to become acquainted with the writings of modern Catholic author Bert Ghezzi. Bert had become my acquisition editor at *Our Sunday Visitor* for a memoir I was to write on my personal journey from Catholicism to atheism to back where I'd started—thank God! As curiosity got the best of me, I researched a bit about Bert and decided to acquire a copy of one of his books, *The Heart of a Saint*.[2]

Almost right off the bat, in chapter two, I was introduced to one St. Aelred of Rievaulx (1110–1167)—a man who so moved Bert, he wrote that his four sons rejoiced that he had named them before he discovered Aelred! Well, Aelred had a great impact on me as well, and my sons could also rejoice that they too had been named long before. I recall that one of the first tidbits about Aelred that intrigued and amused me was his penchant for praying while standing in a pool of frigid water. I knew that my own namesake, St.

1. St. Aelred of Rievaulx, *Spiritual Friendship*, Lawrence C. Braceland, trans., Marsha L. Dutton, ed. (Trappist, KY: Cistercian Publications, 2010).

2. Bert Ghezzi, *The Heart of a Saint: Ten Ways to Grow Closer to God* (Ijamsville, MD: Word Among Us Press, 2007).

Kevin of Glendalough, was fond of doing the same thing, some six hundred years before Aelred's time, in his glen of two lakes a couple of hundred miles to the west, across the Irish Sea.

In his selection of saints for chapter-long biographies, Bert chose St. Aelred to personify the lesson of "Loving Others." It was through that mini-biography that I become aware of and soon devoured Aelred's books *The Mirror of Charity* and, most central to this book's concern, *Spiritual Friendship*. So richly moving and elegantly crafted were Aelred's books that I was amazed that I had never heard of him before. As the years went by and I mentioned his works to many learned Catholics, I discovered I was not alone. I was gratified to find that Aelred's spiritual descendants in his religious order of Cistercians have published many fine books by and about him, but still I hoped I might contribute something about this great saint's ideas, specifically on friendship, which might reach a wide popular audience, and which would include his writings on friendship in the context of, and interaction with, those of Aristotle, Cicero, and St. Thomas Aquinas.

Having tentatively broached the idea to publishers here and there over the years without any real bites, when I came across Angelico Press a few years back I was impressed by the breadth of the subject matter of their books, particularly by books that respectfully addressed and explored the interplay between classical philosophy and Christian theology. Further, they had previously published books by several authors I have the honor of calling friends.[3] Having received their acceptance of my idea for a book on the lessons of the Roman Stoic philosophers, which would become *The Porch and the Cross*,[4] a couple of years later I suggested the concept of this book to Angelico. That it was accepted you have proof in your hands, and I

---

3. Sister Matthew Marie Cummings, O.P. & Sister Elizabeth Anne Allen, O.P. eds., *Behold the Heritage: Foundations of Education in the Dominican Tradition* (Kettering, OH: Angelico Press, 2012); Shane Kapler, *Through, With, and In Him: The Prayer Life of Jesus and How to Make It Our Own* (Kettering, OH: Angelico Press, 2014).

4. Kevin Vost, *The Porch and the Cross: Ancient Catholic Wisdom for Modern Christian Living* (Kettering, OH: Angelico Press, 2014).

heartily thank publisher John Riess and all at Angelico for it. I thank my friend Shane Kapler as well, for writing a right friendly foreword.

As to what, exactly, the concept was—well, we need to move on to the introduction for that.

Introduction:
What This Book is About

After what we have said, a discussion of friendship would naturally follow, since it is an excellence or implies excellence, and is besides most necessary with a view to living. For without friends no one would choose to live, though he had all other goods. . . .

~ Aristotle, *Nicomachean Ethics*, Book VIII, 1[1]

For while you were pleading to me again and again to write something on friendship, the subject appealed to me as both worthy of general study, and well fitted to our intimacy. Therefore I have not been unwilling to benefit the public at your request.

~ Marcus Tullius Cicero, *De Amicitia*, 1, 4[2]

I acquired Cicero's famous book on friendship, and at once it seemed to me both useful in its weighty thoughts and pleasant in its agreeable eloquence.

~ St. Aelred of Rievaulx, *Spiritual Friendship*, Prologue[3]

After the Philosopher has determined the moral and intellectual virtues and continence, which is something imperfect in the genus of virtue, he now turns his attention to friendship which is founded upon virtue as an effect of it.

~ St. Thomas Aquinas, *Commentary on the Nicomachean Ethics*, Book VIII, 1[4]

---

1. Aristotle, *Nicomachean Ethics*, in *The Complete Works of Aristotle*, Jonathan Barnes, ed. (Princeton, NJ: Princeton University Press, 1995), 1825.

2. Cicero, *On Friendship*, W.A. Falconer, trans. (Cambridge, MA: Harvard University Press, 2001), 111.

3. St. Aelred of Rievaulx, *Spiritual Friendship*, Mark F. Williams, trans. (Chicago, IL: University of Scranton Press, 2002), 27.

4. St. Thomas Aquinas, *Commentary on Aristotle's Nicomachean Ethics*, C.I. Litzinger, O.P. trans. (Notre Dame, IN: Dumb Ox Books, 1964), 476.

The Four Friendships: From Aristotle to Aquinas

One Soul within Two Bodies—
Two Times in Sixteen Hundred Years

When I came across St. Aelred's marvelous *De Spirituali Amicitia* (Spiritual Friendship), I had already read Cicero's fine *De Amicitia* (On Friendship), but had no idea that a medieval Christian saint had been so moved by it that it had inspired him to write a classic of his own, one which incorporated many of its ideas and expanded on them in many intriguing and beautiful ways. I was also familiar with Aristotle's magnificent *Nicomachean Ethics,* including its two books (chapters in modern parlance) of ten which were specifically devoted to an examination of friendship. I knew, too, that St. Thomas Aquinas had penned a commentary on every line of "the Philosopher's" (his respectful title for Aristotle) *Nicomachean Ethics,* including, of course, books eight and nine on friendship. Indeed, within his own masterpiece of over 3,000 pages, the *Summa Theologica*, St. Thomas's treatise of over 100 pages on the virtue of charity starts with an examination of charity as a very special kind of friendship, drawing its definition of friendship again from "the Philosopher."

While Cicero (106–43 BC) does not explicitly quote the *Nicomachean Ethics,* he clearly draws from its ideas, possibly as passed down in the writings of Theophrastus (c. 371–287 BC), a student of Aristotle (384–322 BC) and the man to succeed Aristotle as the head of his school, the Lyceum. St. Aelred (AD 1110–1167), as we saw, explicitly cites and incorporates a host of ideas and phrases from the Latin-writing Cicero, but does not cite the Greek-writing Aristotle. St. Thomas Aquinas (AD 1225–1274) relies heavily and openly on Aristotle (accessible to him through translation into Latin), yet, though familiar with Cicero and frequently citing him on other subjects over the course of his analysis of virtues in the *Summa Theologica,* he does not cite *De Amicitia* in his treatments of friendship. Neither does Thomas ever cite St. Aelred. It appears that he was not aware of this Cistercian's writings, though he clearly knew St. Bernard, the man who commissioned St. Aelred's first book, *The Mirror of Charity.*

As we will see shortly, it was proverbial even in Aristotle's day that friends were as "one soul within two bodies." It seems that though they never met on earth and lived 1200 years apart, Cicero and St. Aelred were in some respects such kindred spirits, especially regarding the topic of friendship itself. We see a similar metaphorical sharing of souls in Aristotle and St. Thomas Aquinas, who lived nearly 1600 years apart. These two unique "friendships" supply the grist for the mill of this book, *The Four Friendships*. The *four* refers to these four men's unique but overlapping writings on *friendship itself*.

The title, as you might surmise, is also a nod to modern Christian author C. S. Lewis (1898–1963), the author of *The Four Loves*. In this book, Lewis expounded upon four human "loves," these being affection, erotic love, friendship, and charity. Here, our focus will rest squarely upon friendship, though the other kinds of love will certainly be considered for their potential bearing upon friendship, most particularly charity in the second half of this book.

Literature, Lessons, and Legacies

THE FOUR main writings which we will address in the pages ahead are very interesting pieces of *literature* in themselves—books of enduring value with pleasing, though different, styles, from the methodical lectures of the encyclopedic Aristotle to the stately quasi-dialogue of the noble Cicero, from the intimate dialogue of St. Aelred (itself a dazzling display of friendship in action) to the formal scholastic disputations from the angelic intellect of St. Thomas Aquinas. In chapters 1, 3, 5, and 7 of this book, I will provide abridgements or summaries of these great works, at times with direct quotations from modern translations of the Greek of Aristotle or the Latin of Cicero, Aelred, and Thomas. I also had access to the original Greek or Latin versions for all but St. Aelred, in whose case I availed myself of three modern English translations that are referenced within the text. My hope is that every reader's appetite will be whetted to taste firsthand from these great literary feasts, having nibbled on the appetizers herein.

The main goals of this book, however, concern the next two letter "ls"—*lessons* and *legacies*, that is. The abridgements and summaries in chapters 1, 3, 5, and 7 are presented to provide a taste not so much of these great author's literary styles as of the *lessons* they teach. You will find very little commentary in those chapters, as I have striven to let these great thinkers both think and speak for themselves. My own thoughts are proffered in later chapters, after the reader has had time to think over the lessons himself.[5]

This leads us to their great *legacies*. Aristotle wrote in an earlier chapter of the same *Nicomachean Ethics* that "the object of our inquiry is not to know what virtue is but how to become good...."[6] So, too, we will examine these four writings on friendship not merely as works of literature or historical curiosities, but as practical guides to us as we seek to build, maintain, and enjoy friendships of our own today. *The object of our inquiry, then, is not to know what friendship is, but how to become good friends.*

In chapters 2, 4, 6, and 8 you will find my own commentary as well a sampling of the great legacies across the centuries in which other thinkers, secular philosophers and Christian theologians, have reflected upon the lessons they learned from these four great and foundational friends of friendship. For readers heretofore unfamiliar with these writings on friendship, I imagine that many new vistas will be opened regarding the breadth, depth, and nature of this uniquely human and perennially important topic. I hope, as well, that it will inspire all readers to better understand, appreciate, and live out *the friendships in their own lives*, as we address issues including the following through the eyes of two sages and two saints:

- What is friendship?
- What are the *three kinds of friendship* discussed for over two millennia?

---

5. I hope many "herselves" are among my readers too. I will often use masculine pronouns in this book because the authors themselves did so, but the general principles of friendship examined within this book certainly apply to females as well, in terms of both male-female and female-female friendships. We will look at such things in more depth in a few chapters.

6. Aristotle, *Nicomachean Ethics*, in Aristotle, *On Man in the Universe*, James E. C. Welldon, trans. (New York: Walter J. Black, Inc., 1943), 103.

• Is there only one "true," "complete," "primary," "perfect," or "genuine" friendship?

• What are the *five key things* people wish for and do for their friends?

• What has friendship to do with relatives, with husbands and wives, fellow travelers, business associates, teammates, fellow citizens, and systems of government?

• What behaviors are most harmful to friendship?

• When should the bonds of friendship be severed?

• What is the relationship between friendship and virtue?

• How do we make ourselves more suitable for friendship?

• Do those who love themselves most make the *worst* or the *best* of friends?

• Is it better *to love* a friend or to *be loved*?

• How does the special focus of friendship square with the Christian call to love *everyone* in charity?

• Can we truly be friends with God?

Ancient Greeks and Romans Bearing Gifts: Medieval Monks and Mendicants Improving Them

I will note as well a similarity to and a difference from my previous book on the Stoics. I believed that the profound psychological and ethical lessons of the Stoics regarding the controlling of emotions and the pursuit of virtue would be helpful to modern Christians, as some of their most valuable ancient ideas, gleaned with their God-given powers of reason, seem to have been forgotten over time.[7] It was one of my pleasant surprises in writing that book to find that one of the early Roman Stoics, Musonius Rufus, teacher of the great Epictetus, wrote so magnificently about the value of human life,

---

7. As I detailed in *The Porch and the Cross*, their seminal ideas on the importance of attitudes and beliefs on emotions and behavior would not be fully incorporated into modern psychotherapy until the 1950s and 1960s. In the Middle Ages, some Christian theologians were so taken with the value of Epictetus's ethical writings that they "Christianized" his *Enchiridon* or *Handbook* as a guidebook for monks. Indeed, three different Christian adaptations are still extant.

marriage, and the family in ways consonant with modern Catholic social teaching that I would dub him a "profound pro-life, pagan philosopher."

I believe that in this book, too, modern Christian readers will find plenty of practical value in these writings of the pagan philosophers Aristotle and Cicero. Still—though I leave it to the reader to judge for himself—I will aver that Sts. Aelred and Thomas Aquinas have not merely appropriated and adapted these ancient pagan philosophical works, but have *elevated and transformed* them most sublimely, bringing the understanding—and hopefully the practice—of friendship to previously unimagined heights of truth, beauty, and goodness, showing how human relations can indeed be Divine.

As I said, I will let you decide about that. In any event, let's begin.

PART I

Aristotle of Stagira's
Virtuous Friendship

✛

Among all the relics of Greek antiquity, Aristotle's Ethics is one of those that retain their interest most freshly. To many readers, new to this kind of study, its application of rigorous logical analysis to the problem of conduct comes as a revelation.

        ⌐H. Rackham, in *The Nicomachean Ethics*[1]

---

1. Aristotle, *The Nicomachean Ethics*, H. Rackham, trans. (Cambridge, MA: Harvard University Press, 1999), xxvii.

1

Virtuous Friendship
in the *Nicomachean Ethics*

But complete friendship is the friendship of those who are good and alike in point of virtue. For such people wish in similar fashion for the good things for each other insofar as they are good, and they are good in themselves. But those who wish for the good things for their friends, for their friends' sake, are friends most of all.

⁓Aristotle, *Nicomachean Ethics*, Book 8, chapter 3[1]

IN THIS CHAPTER I will provide summaries of books 8 and 9 of Aristotle's *Nicomachean Ethics,* the books—"chapters," in modern parlance—that specifically address friendship. Context and commentary will come in chapter 2; here I will try to cut to the chase and let readers dig straight into the world of Aristotelian friendship. I have provided lengthier summaries of book 8 and briefer summaries for the chapters of book 9 to keep this chapter of reasonable length and, hopefully, to entice readers to read Aristotle's own complete text. In composing these summaries I had access to Aristotle's Greek text through the Loeb Classical Library edition from Harvard University Press, as well as six English translations.[2]

1. Aristotle's *Nicomachean Ethics,* Robert C. Bartlett & Susan D. Collins, trans. (Chicago: University of Chicago Press, 2011), 168. The authors include a footnote that an alternative translation for Aristotle's *teleia,* rendered "complete," would be "perfect."

2. *The Complete Works of Aristotle: The Revised Oxford Edition,* Jonathan Barnes, ed. Vol. I (Princeton, NJ: Princeton University Press, 1984); the Bartlett & Collins translation cited above; St. Thomas Aquinas, *Commentary on Aristotle's Nicomachean Ethics,* C. I. Litzinger, O.P. trans. (Notre Dame, IN: Dumb Ox Books,

A variety of important words have more than one possible translation, as our first footnote in this chapter has already made clear. In these instances, I have not always been consistent, having sometimes used one option and at other times another, or perhaps even two together, to hopefully provide a greater chance that one or the other might strike individual readers as particularly significant. Some of these choices will be made clear in our next chapter.

I will conclude by noting that the subheadings for each of the chapters are not in the original. They are my own contributions, aimed to emphasize key concepts and to aid readers in going back and tracking down ideas of interest, either in this text or in the originals. I will also at times italicize statements that were particularly striking to me, and I likewise invite you to be on the lookout for statements that you yourself find especially meaningful or useful.

With that said, let us journey to 4th century BC Athens and let the man whom Dante Alighieri called "the master of those who know"[3] tell us what he knows of friendship.

Nicomachean Ethics: Book VIII Abridgement

1. Friends: Who Needs Them?

Having addressed fundamental issues of ethics—including the nature of happiness and its ultimate value, along with the virtues necessary to attain it—in seven books and more than one hundred pages, Aristotle draws our attention in books eight and nine to the value and nature of friendship. Friendship, he tells us, either is or implies arête (virtue or excellence) and is so necessary to living that no one would choose to live without it even if he had everything else he needed.

1964); *Aristotle: On Man In The Universe*, Louise Ropes Loomis, ed. (New York: Walter Black Co., 1943); *Aristotle Nicomachean Ethics*, second ed., Terrence Irwin, trans. (Indianapolis, IN: Hackett Publishing Co., 1999); *Aristotle XIX: Nicomachean Ethics*, H. Rackham, trans. (Cambridge, MA: Harvard University Press [1926], 1999).

3. *Inferno*, 4.131.

Aristotle then elaborates on why all who would live the good life need friends. The rich and the holders of powerful positions need friends even more than others, since what is more desirable and worthy of praise than being able to use our prosperity to benefit those most dear to us? Further, friends help guard and protect our positions and property. As for the poor and those who suffer misfortunes, friends may be their only refuge.

The young need friends to keep them on the right path in life, and the old need friends to help them cope with physical frailty. Those in the prime of life need friends, too, for friends stir each other toward nobler actions, and "when two go together..."[4] they are better able to comprehend and act in difficult situations.

Parents seem to have a natural desire for friendship with their children—a tendency observable not only among humans, but among birds and most animals. Friendship is desired by members of the same species, and foremost by human beings, which is why we praise humanitarians or philanthropists. When we travel, we see how dear men are to their fellow men everywhere throughout the world.

Friendship bonds states together, and lawmakers value it even over justice, for unanimity or harmony within a city is like the harmony of friendship, and when people are friends there is no need of justice in addition to it—though those who are just still need friends. Indeed, justice in its ultimate form has the qualities of friendship.

Now, friendship is not only *necessary*, it is also *noble*. We praise those who love their friends, and it is thought a fine thing to have many friends.

As to disputed points about the nature of friendships and what moves us to toward particular people as potential friends, some say "birds of a feather flock together" and "like is drawn to like," while others say "two of a trade will never agree," suggesting that "opposites attract." This is the realm of natural science rather than ethics,

---

4. Here Aristotle references Homer's *Iliad*, Book X, 224, where Diomedes seeks a companion to join him in attacking the Trojan camp.

and will not be considered in any depth here.[5] What will be considered are issues related to moral character and human passions, such as whether friendships can be formed between any people, whether wicked people can be friends, and whether there are different kinds of friendship.

2. The Three Causes of Love

We are attracted with love toward things that are *good* or *pleasant* as ends in themselves, and toward things that are *useful* as means to attaining those ends. We must consider, as well, whether we love what is *good in itself*, or what is *good for us*. Sometimes these are not the same, and this also applies to pleasant things. Still, this is not really an issue for our concern, because *what is lovable is what seems lovable to us.*

Now, with these three motives of love made clear (i.e., the good, the pleasant, & the useful), we must note that we do not properly apply the word "love" to our feelings toward inanimate objects. We don't truly "love" wine, for example, because wine cannot love us in return, and because it would be ridiculous to wish the wine's own good. We want wine to stay good so that we may enjoy drinking it! Everyone knows though that we ought to wish our friends well *for their own sakes.* When we wish people well in this sense it is called *benevolence* or *good will*, and when they return good will toward us, *this reciprocal benevolence is what we call friendship.*

Further, this mutual good will must be recognized. We may wish well others whom we have not seen, but there is no true friendship unless this benevolence is known to both parties. So then, to be friends, people must wish each other well, each must be aware of the other's feelings, and the feelings must arise from the aforementioned reasons of goodness, pleasure, or usefulness.

---

5. Aristotle briefly mentions Euripides, for example, who said that "the parched earth loves the rain," suggesting attraction between opposites, Heraclitus, who, on a similar note said that "from different notes come the fairest tune," while Empedocles argued to the contrary, that similar aims at similar.

3. The Three Kinds of Friendship

As the reasons for loving and friendship differ in kind, so too are there three different kinds of friendship. People who love each other wish well to each other in a way that corresponds to their manner of loving. So in *friendships of utility,* friends love each other not for themselves, but for the benefits they derive from each other. The same holds for *friendships of pleasure;* friends love witty people, for example, not for their character, but because they find the witty pleasant. These kinds of friends love the other *not for what the other is in himself,* but only because they are useful or pleasant *to them.* These kinds of friendships are incidental only, since the friends do not love each other for who they are, but as instruments for utility or pleasure. They are also often short-lived, since these friends quickly part ways if one finds the other no longer amusing or helpful.

The relatively superficial and fleeting friendships of utility are common among the elderly who seek out assistance or profit rather than pleasure and among youths and those in the prime of life who are especially ambitious regarding their own interests. Such friends do not typically live together or spend a lot of time together, for they may not find each other's company pleasant. They get together at the times they can be of use to each other, and at those times they may share the kind of pleasure that rests in the hopes of what they imagine they might gain from each other. A similar kind of friendship is found among host and guests.

Friendships of pleasure are found most commonly among young people, since they are driven by passions and the desire for immediate sensual gratification. As they grow older, their sources of pleasure shift quickly, as do the friendships based on them. Youths are prone to intense, amorous feelings as well, and, being based on emotion and pleasure, they too may quickly shift as they rapidly fall in and out of love—perhaps even several times in a single day! Those involved in friendships of pleasure do, indeed, seek out each other's company—while the pleasure lasts.

The only *perfect* friendships, however, are *friendships of virtue,* founded upon the goodness each friend finds in and wishes for the other. These friends love their friends and wish them well *for their friends' own sake.* This friendship is not incidental like the others,

19

and it is the truest form of friendship because it entails *love of the friend for who he is, for his virtuous character,* rather than perhaps ephemeral accidents, like his wit or wealth. Such friendships are far more likely to endure and become permanent, because they contain within them *all* of the elements of the other kinds of friendship as well. Good people are not only good in themselves, but are glad to be useful, helping their friends and bringing good things their way. Virtuous friends bring pleasure to one another as well, for every virtuous person finds pleasure in his own actions and in the deeds of his friend. Virtuous people act in similar ways, doing the same kinds of good deeds.

Perfect friendships, in light of their excellence, are likely to be rare, for truly virtuous people are rare. Further, such friends need time together to grow familiar, as the proverb relates that people cannot really know each other until they have "eaten salt together" over the course of many meals and found each other lovable and worthy of trust. *The desire to become friends may arise in an instant, but true friendship must build over time.*

4. The Friendships Compared and Contrasted

The incomplete friendships of utility or pleasure are most likely to be long-lasting when the friends get the same thing from each other and from the same source—for example, when the witty take pleasure in each other's banter, in contrast to erotic friendships wherein one lover takes pleasure from seeing his beloved, while the beloved takes pleasure in being the object of attention. When the bloom of youthful beauty fades from the beloved, the friendship fades as well, for the lover no longer derives pleasure from sight of the beloved, and the beloved no longer receives the lover's attention. Many of these people remain friends nonetheless, because they see similar natural dispositions in each other and grow accustomed to them over time.

Friendships based on utility as opposed to pleasure are even more likely to be fleeting, because such friendships are quick to dissolve when the friends find they are no longer of use to one another. This is the lowest form of friendship because the friends are not lovers of one another, but of their own profit.

In pursuit of pleasure or utility, bad people may seek each other out as friends, good people might befriend bad ones, and those neither good nor bad might befriend someone with any kind of character. Only good people can love their friends for their own sakes, for bad people do not take delight in others unless it brings them some advantage.

Further, only virtuous friendships are immune to the assaults of slander, for good people will not be quick to believe ill of people who have proven to them over time of their character and trustworthiness. The lesser kinds of friendships lacking in virtue do nothing to prevent the kind of suspicion and mistrust that may serve to dissolve them.

Still, people do use the word "friends" to describe those who associate due to utility—for example, states are often said to be "friendly allies" when each seeks advantage from the other. Still, it is only the good who can obtain complete and perfect friendship—that which is based on virtue and which incorporates pleasure and usefulness. Friendships of utility or pleasure alone are only called *friendships* because they dimly resemble true and virtuous friendship.

5. Friendship in Act and Habit

When speaking of excellences or of virtues in general, some people are called *good* because of their habits or ongoing states of character, while others are called *good* because of the particular virtuous acts they perform. It is the same in friendship; true friends remain so even while asleep or separated by distance, because the ongoing disposition to be friends is still within them. Still, if absence is prolonged without opportunity for friendly interaction, friendships may easily dissolve, a truth which has been captured by the proverb "out of sight, out of mind."

Old people and sour people are little prone to friendship because they tend not to be pleasant. It is human nature to avoid what is painful and seek out what is pleasant.

People who get along with one another but do not live together or interact regularly seem to be *well-wishers* rather than friends, for nothing befits friendship as living and spending time together. While those in need desire company, even the blessedly happy who have everything they need seek out companionship daily, and a life of solitude suits such people least of all.

Love or affection seems to be an act, while friendship is a state or habit, for we may feel affection for lifeless objects, but the mutual love of friendship requires choice and choices spring from habitual states, so that virtuous people wish well to their friends not according to passing feelings, but according to the virtuous habits they have developed over time.

6. Additional Characteristics of the Three Kinds of Friendship

The reason why elderly and sour people are less likely to form friendships is that they are more ill-tempered and less likely to seek out companionship with others, for the actions most conducive to friendship are a good temper and the ability to enjoy interaction with others. This is why the young tend to form friends quickly while the old do not. Youths tend to delight in friendly interactions. The old and those often in bad moods might wish others well, but they do not seek out the togetherness that true friendship requires.

We cannot have complete and true friendship with a great number of people, just as we cannot be in love with many people at the same time, because true friendship, like erotic love, is like an excess, and can only be appropriately directed toward a single person. We cannot fully please many people at the same time, or even be a good to them, if we spread out our love or our friendship too thin, having too little time to become familiar with our friend or lover and grow in shared experience.

Friendships of pleasure are more like real friendship than friendships of utility, because these friends get the same things from each other and delight each other for the same reasons. These friendships are marked by generosity and are common among the young. Friendships of utility are especially suited to the commercially-minded. Fortunate people may have no need for friendships of utility, but they still seek out pleasant interactions with others, and the wise among them will seek out friends who are not only pleasant, but virtuous.

People holding positions of power and authority often seek out separate classes of friends; friends they seek out who are of use for their purposes, and friends who are pleasant to them. It is rare that the same person will be a friend of both pleasure and use, because, though virtuous people are both pleasant and useful, they rarely become friends with those in superior positions unless the superior is also superior in virtue. Superiority in both power and virtue is quite rarely found.

To recap, *friendships of utility and pleasure* do involve *equality* in that the concerned parties get similar things from one another, and virtuous friendships do include qualities of *usefulness and pleasure.* Such relationships therefore may be termed *friendships* in a limited sense, although they lack the *completeness, stability, and relative permanence* that we find in *friendships of virtue.*

7. Friendship between Unequals

There is another kind of friendship that involves inequality, such as that of a father for his son, any older person for any younger person, a husband for his wife, or a ruler for his subject. These friendships differ from one another because the excellence and function of each is different, and each arises from a different way of loving. Neither party gets the same thing from the other, nor should they seek it. When children render to their parents what is due them as those who brought them into the world, and when parents render what is due to their children as their offspring, their friendship will be lasting and good.

In all friendships of unequal relations, the love should be *proportional*—in other words, the superior person should receive more love than he or she gives, because he or she provides greater benefits to the other. In that way, when the lesser party gives more love to the party who provides greater benefits, a kind of equality is achieved that is appropriate to friendship. When a great difference in virtue, vice, wealth, or anything else develops between friends, however, such persons will no longer maintain their friendship or even expect to do so. We see this most clearly in the case of the gods, for they surpass us so far in all things. The rule also applies in the cases of kings and of the best and wisest of men; base men cannot expect to be their friends.

The fact that the vast difference in excellence between a god and a

23

human precludes friendship between the two gives rise to a question on the nature of true friendships. If friends truly wish the best for their friends, would they wish them to attain the greatest of goods and become gods, thus losing their friendship with them? Well, if a friend wishes good things to his friend *as to another self*, the friend must remain as he is, a man. Hence it appears that friends will wish each other good things, but not necessarily all the greatest things, because each person wishes good things most of all for himself.

8. On Loving and Being Loved in Friendships

Many people are driven by ambition to prefer being loved to loving. This is why they love flatterers who pretend to love them more than they are loved, feeling themselves thereby honored and esteemed. *Friendship, though, consists more in loving than in being loved.* Consider the enjoyment a mother derives from loving, so that some mothers are willing to give up their children to be raised by others and are happy just to know their child is thriving, even if they are unable to see the child and receive its love in return. Since friendship consists in loving rather than in being loved, and people who love their friends are praised, *loving seems to be the hallmark excellence of friends, and only friendships that display such love are lasting.*

It is because of this central importance of loving that unequals can be friends. They are equalized by the outpouring of love. Equality and likeness are essential to friendship, and especially likeness in virtue, since the virtuous hold fast to their virtue and neither ask nor grant their friend's base services. *Virtuous people do not do bad things and do not permit their friends to do so either.* Vicious people, on the contrary, are inconstant and unsteady even in their own characters and do not remain friends for long. They may befriend each other for a short time while they enjoy each other's vices. Useful or pleasant friends last longer, as long as they provide each other with benefits or pleasures.

The friendship that arises most often among opposites are the friendships of utility which we find between the poor and the rich, the ignorant and the learned, for what people lack they aim to attain by offering something different in return. Friendships between lovers and their beloveds, and between the beautiful and the ugly, appear to also be examples. It would seem, in such cases, that the friends are not so much seeking their contrary as striving to achieve some state in the middle, but such concerns takes us beyond the scope of this discussion and may be dismissed.

9. Friendship within Communities

As stated at the beginning of our examination, friendship and justice deal with the same topics and are found in the same people. Every community exhibits some form of both justice and friendship. As soldiers and fellow-travelers associate in communion, we see that the extent of their friendship is also the extent of the justice found between them. The proverb "What friends have is in common" is true, for friendship depends on community.

While brothers and companions have everything in common, members of other communities will vary in the extent to which they share things in common, since some friendships are closer than others. The claims of justice vary according to the nature of the friendship, so that they are not the same between parents and children, nor between close companions or fellow citizens. There is a difference, too, between acts of injustice, since unjust actions are worse when perpetrated on closer friends. It is more heinous to rob a close companion than another citizen, or to fail to help a brother rather than a stranger, and more terrible to strike one's father than anybody else. The demands of justice naturally rise with the closeness of friendship.

All forms of community are like parts of the political community, since all people band together for some kind of mutual advantage. This is the aim of the political community, for when legislators aim at the common good of all, this is said to be just. Smaller communities, be they groups of soldiers, members of tribes, neighborhoods, religious organizations, or social clubs, all band together in companionship for some good common to the whole group, and not merely for the benefit of the individual. All these groups, then, are types of communities, and *the types of communities will have implications for the types of friendships within them.*

10. Political Systems and Friendships in Households

In considering friendships within political communities, we note there are three types of political systems and three variations that are perversions or corruptions of them. The three systems are *kingship, aristocracy,* and a third based on property qualifications, which can be called *timocracy* (from *timema* for property) but which is usually called *polity.* The best of these three is kingship and the worst timocracy.

The perversion of kingship is *tyranny,* and though both kingship and tyranny are monarchies, they have the greatest difference between them, as between the best and the worst. A true king is self-sufficient and surpasses his subjects in excellence; needing nothing from others, he looks out for the welfare of his people rather than his self-interest, which is the mark of the tyrant. A bad king becomes a tyrant.

The perversion of aristocracy, the rule of the *best* people, is *oligarchy,* the rule of *a few* people, who, lacking in virtue, distribute the goods of the city not fairly to all, but to themselves as they strive to amass great wealth.

The perversion of timocracy is *democracy,* and is but a slight change, for in both rule is held by the populace, but while a timocracy holds property-holders equal, in democracy all are held equal regardless of merit.

A similar pattern can be found within communities found in households, for a father is like a king in his authority over and concern for his children. Indeed, that is why Homer calls Zeus "father," since kingship is fatherly rule. The Persian father, however, acts as a tyrant, treating his children as slaves to serve his own purposes. The friendship of husband and wife is aristocratic, for the man rules by merit in matters pertaining to him, but delegates to the woman the matters fitting for her rule. When the man dominates in all areas, he has become like an oligarch, for he does not acknowledge his wife's own merit. Lastly, we see timocracy among brothers, since they are equal but for age; if there is too great a gap in their ages, their friendship is no longer of the fraternal type. As for democracy, this pattern prevails in households without a master, or in those with such a weak master that everyone does as he pleases.

11. Justice and Friendship in the Political Systems

Each political system involves friendship to the extent that it involves justice. A king is friendly to his subjects through the great benefits and care he provides for their well-being, as a shepherd does for his sheep. This is why Homer called Agamemnon "shepherd of the peoples." The friendship of a father is similar, yet he provides even greater benefits by producing his children's very existence, along with their nurture and training. Ancestors, too, are honored over descendants, all of these being examples of friendships of superiority of one party over the other, wherein justice entails that the inferior party honor the superior party for the benefits bestowed.

The justice within the friendship of man and woman is akin to that of aristocracy where, in accordance with excellence, the better party gets more of what is good, but both receive the good that is proportional to their excellence. The justice in friendship of brothers is like that of close companions of similar age and character, which resembles timocracy, wherein citizens are expected to be equal and fair, ruling in turn and on equal terms.

Justice is hardly to be found in the deviant forms, however, and neither is friendship. They exist least in tyranny. There can be no friendship in tyranny, where the ruler and the ruled share nothing in common, and no justice either, since the relationship is like that between a craftsman and tool, soul and body, master and slave. All the benefit is provided by the latter for the former. In the same way, there can be no true friendship between humans and horses or oxen, nor between a man and a slave *in that he is a slave*, though there can be friendship with a slave *in that he is a human being. Every human being owes justice in some manner to every other human being.* Every human being can participate in some manner in any system of law, and *friendship can therefore exist between any human beings by virtue of the fact that they are human beings.* Hence, while friendships and justice are hardly to be found in tyrannies, they exist to a much greater extent in democracies, where the people are equals and hold much in common.

12. The Kinds of Friendship within Families

While all friendships involve some form of association in community, we note a distinction between friendships of kin and those between companions. The friendships of citizens, tribesmen, fellow travelers, and perhaps those of host and guest resemble friendships of association because they involve some sort of agreement.

The friendship within families seems to be of many kinds, but *they all appear to depend on parental friendship,* for parents love their children as *parts of themselves,* while children love their parents because they consider themselves as *coming from them,* their parents being *the authors of their being.* Parents know better that their children have come from them than children know that they have come from their parents, and a person is more attached to what comes from him as his own (be it a tooth or hair or anything), but that which comes from him may regard him less, if at all. Time produces a similar result in favor of parental love, in that parents love their children as soon as they are born, while the children have to acquire understanding or at least perception before they can love their parents in return. For these same reasons, mothers love their children more than fathers do.

Parents love their children as they love themselves, because what comes from them is like *a second self,* while children love their parents as having come from them and love their siblings as having come from the same parents. Siblings share this same relation to their parents which makes them "of the same blood," or "of the same stock." Indeed, they are, in a sense, the same thing in different individuals. Because they are raised together, familiarity contributes to friendship, for "two of an age get on well together" so that the friendship of siblings is like that of close comrades.

Cousins and other kin are like siblings in that they descend from ancestors who were siblings, with some more closely related to others depending on how near or distant the ancestor is to them.

The friendship of children to parents is like that of men to gods in that they both involve a relation toward what is good and superior. Parents confer the greatest goods on their children by giving them life, ongoing care, and education, and because of their life in common, they also provide more things of use and pleasure than friends who are not related.

The friendship of siblings is similar to that found between companions, especially when their comrades are virtuous and when they are similar to one another. Because they grow in love for each other from birth, come from the same parents, and are raised together in a similar way, their friendships prove most reliable and enduring when tested over time.

It is in the nature of men and women to form friendships as couples. Indeed, *the inclination to form couples is even stronger than that to form cities.* The household comes before the city and is more necessary, and reproduction is found in all animals, including man. Human beings, however, live together not merely for childbearing as other animals do, but for all the various goods in life, and for this reason, functions are divided between the man and the woman, so that both might contribute the best of their gifts for the family's common good. This is why we find both pleasure and utility in the friendship within couples, and if they are excellent people, these friendships based on virtue will produce mutual delight as they enjoy one another's moral goodness. Children provide the bonds for these unions, which is why childless couples are more likely to separate, for children are a common good to both and common goods hold people together.

How man and wife—and, more generally speaking, any friend and another friend—*ought to behave toward each other* is really the same question as *how they are to live their lives justly,* and what is just will vary according to relationship, for we do not seem to have the same duties toward a friend, a stranger, a companion, and a classmate.

13. Conflicts and Quarrels in Friendships between Equals

There are three kinds of friendship, as we noted early on, and within each kind some are friendships between equals and others involve some inequality with some manner of superiority and inferiority between the friends. Not only can equally good people become friends, but a better person can befriend a worse one, and there may also be either equality or inequality in friendships of utility or pleasure. As this is the case, in friendships of equals the friends must be equal in the love they share and in everything else, while in friendships of unequals each must return to their friend in proportion to superior merits.

Conflicts and quarrels arise only or chiefly in friendships of utility, as might be expected. In virtuous friendships, each friend is eager to benefit the other, and people are not likely to complain when others love and care for them; if they are gracious, they will strive to return the like. The man who excels and gives more will not complain about his friend, because he still gets what he aims for in the giving of benefits, and both desire the good.

There are few conflicts in friendships of pleasure, either, because both parties get what they want if they enjoy spending their time together, and it would appear ridiculous if a friend complained that the other did not give him pleasure, since he is free to part company with the friend if he does not find his company pleasant.

Friendships of utility are bound to be rife with complaints, since the friends use each other for gain. Always seeking for more, thinking they have not received their fair share, they chastise their friends for giving them less than they desire and deserve. The friend who serves them can never help them as much as they would like.

There would seem to be two kinds of justice, one unwritten and the other legal, and similarly, *two kinds of friendship of utility*, one *moral* and the other *legal*. Problems frequently arise when people do not dissolve their friendships in the same kind of utility as when they formed them. *Legal* friendships are based on fixed terms, and the more commercial or mercenary type requires immediate payment, while the more liberal or generous kind expects repayments, but does not set fixed time limits or terms for them. *Moral* friendships of utility are not based on explicit terms of repayment. Such a friend offers a present or service of some kind to a friend, but he expects that he will receive back as much or more, so what he offers is truly no gift, but a loan, and he will complain if he is not paid back. This happens because most people *approve of* what is fine or noble, but *choose* what is in their own self-interest, and while it is *noble* to help a friend with no aim at a reward, it is seen as *beneficial to oneself* to receive one.

Therefore, if we can return the equivalent of what we have received from some person who seeks to be our friend, we should do so, but we should be careful not to accept benefits from those unwilling to be our friends, and to make explicit plans to repay the other if we have accepted the benefit. It is disputable whether we should weigh a service rendered by its usefulness to the recipient and return in that measure, or whether we should weigh it by its cost to the benefactor. For a recipient says that what he got was a small matter for the giver, that he could have gotten it somewhere else, and this belittles the service; the giver, on the contrary, says it was the greatest thing he had, that no one else could provide it, or that it was given at a time of danger or similar need. Now, if the friendship aims at *utility,* then *the true measure is the advantage it provides to the recipient.* For it is the recipient who has asked for the service, and the giver provides the service assuming he will receive the equivalent. Therefore, the recipient should return as great a benefit as he has received—and more, if he is noble.

In virtuous friendships, such disputes do not arise because the free decision of the giver is like the measure, since choice is the essential element in virtue and character.

14. Conflicts and Quarrels in Friendships between Unequals

Conflicts also arise in friendships in which one party is superior to the other, for each person expects to receive more than the other, and friendships are ended when this happens. Better people think they are entitled to more by virtue of their goodness, and more beneficial people think likewise. Benefactors think a person should not get an equal share of things if he is useless, otherwise the relationship is more public service than friendship. In this view, friendships are like business ventures, and those who contribute more should get more in return. The less useful friend, however, holds the opposite view, that a virtuous friend should rightly help his needy friends. Otherwise, what is the use of a good or powerful friend if you have nothing to gain from him?

In any event, each party would seem to be correct that each one should get more out of the friendship than the other, *but not more of the same thing.* The superior person should obtain more *honor* and the inferior person should get more *gain*, for honor is the prize of virtue and kindness, while gain provides assistance to the needy. We see this, as well, in political systems, because honor is not given to the man who contributes nothing to the good of the community; what belongs to the community is given to the man who benefits it, and honor is something the community can give in common. It is impossible to make money off the community and at the same time be honored, for nobody wants a smaller share in *all* things, so the person who willingly loses wealth for the community's sake is honored and the person who is willing to receive gifts in office receives wealth but forfeits honor. Thus, the distribution of rewards is proportional to merit, and friendship is preserved.

This, then, is how we should deal with unequals; the person who receives benefits in wealth or excellence must give honor to his benefactor or superior, repaying *as best as he can.* Friendship demands only what a person *can do,* and does not ask to return what accords with the worth of benefits offered, when it is impossible. For example, who can ever pay honor to the gods or to their parents that equal the benefits they have given them? Still, the person who aims to serve them to the best of his powers is thought to be virtuous.

This is why a person should never disown his father, though fathers may disown sons, for the son is always in debt to his father for the life he has received from him. Creditors can remit debts, though, and a father can do so too. Still, we presume that no father would repudiate a son who was not extremely wicked, for, apart from their natural friendship, it is human nature not to refuse help to others. But if a son is truly vicious, he will naturally avoid caring for his father, or will do it half-heartedly, for many people want to receive benefits and yet avoid offering benefits if they think that it will bring them no profit. So much, then, for these questions.

So much then, too, for such detailed presentations of Aristotle's chapters within book eight. In completing this chapter, we will move next into short and sweet summaries in this author's words of the remaining twelve chapters in Aristotle's book nine, the last of the two that he devoted to friendship within the *Nicomachean Ethics.* Having set the stage with examples of Aristotle's nuanced reasoning regarding each issue, we will now strive to cut to the chase, ferreting out just a few of the key ideas within each chapter, some of which we'll address in more depth in our first legacy chapter.

Nicomachean Ethics: Book IX Epitomes

1. Friends Who Want Different Things (and the Value of Philosophy)

Digging deeper into the common reasons friends quarrel and friendships end, Aristotle concludes that differences arise when friends get back from each other something other than what they desire, *because getting what you do not desire is like not getting anything.* He retells the amusing story of a man who offered to reward a lyre-player with a greater reward the better he played. In the morning, when the musician asked for his reward, the man replied that he exchanged pleasure for pleasure (in giving the musician the pleasure of anticipating a reward, and perhaps the pleasure of his own excellent performance!).[6]

As for the true worth of a benefit that a giver gives, Aristotle relates the story of Protagoras, who, after teaching, would ask his pupils to estimate the value of what he taught, then charge them accordingly. After a brief attack on the Sophists,[7] arguing that no one would pay them anything for what they *really* know, Aristotle observes that those who share true philosophy with us have provided something so worthy that it cannot be measured in money or repaid with enough honor. Indeed, those who help us attain wisdom and virtue grant us such a great boon that we must return to them the best that we can, as we would to our parents and the gods!

---

6. Alas, this old trick calls to mind one I would use on my students years ago. While teaching B. F. Skinner's behavioral psychology of reinforcement and punishment, I would sometimes offer students a great reward if they could answer a question I posed them. When someone answered correctly, I would clap and say, "Good job!"—the perhaps-disappointing reward being what Skinner called *verbal positive reinforcement* (though if overused, such antics could have a punishing effect and making question-answering behavior *less likely!*).

7. These were professional rhetoricians for hire who taught ways to win arguments through clever but false means, as is captured in the English word "sophistry" that they inspired.

2. Conflicts in the Duties of Friendship

Here Aristotle examines several potential conflicts involving different kind of friendship, including whether the special status of a
friend can trump our obligations to others. He concludes that while
we owe friends special respect, and our fathers the most respect of
all, generally speaking we should repay services others have done for
us before we grant favors to friends, just as we should pay our debts
to our creditors before we give out loans to our friends, though
there may be exceptions in extreme circumstances. Everyone should
be rendered his due, though not everyone can claim the same
respect. Though a father can claim the highest respect, he cannot
claim unlimited respect, since Zeus himself does not expect unlimited sacrifices. Still, we must strive to bestow to each class of friend
the respect that is natural and fitting for them, with special duties
toward our parents. We should show respect, as well, to all elders by
doing things such as standing to receive them and offering them
seats at the head of the table. Respect is also due to our companions
and brothers, distant kin, fellow citizens, and everyone else, as we
consider their nearness to us, their character, and the good they
have done for us.

3. On Ending Friendships

Now Aristotle addresses the question of whether or not we ought to
end friendship with people when their character has changed. This
should be no problem in friendships of utility or pleasure. It is reasonable that the friendship should cease when one party is no longer
pleasant or useful to the other. It is problematic, however, if a friend
loved us for utility or pleasure while he pretended to love us for our
character. In such cases, a man must blame himself if the friend
made no pretense about the true nature of the friendship, but he can
complain if the other deceived him. We justly complain about counterfeit money, and friendship is more valuable than money.

A more troubling issue arises when a person who was loved for
his goodness has turned bad. This renders love impossible, for only
the good is truly lovable. Still, the friendship need not be ended at
once if there is any chance for a cure of the friend's descent into
vice. Indeed, we should try to help protect and restore a friend's

character even more than we would his property, but it is proper to end the friendship if attempts to restore the friend's character fail.

Friendships may also end when one friend grows greatly in virtue and opens a wide gap in the excellence the friends once shared, so that they no longer esteem and enjoy the same things. Even so, when such friendships end, the former friend should not be forgotten, and consideration should be given to him over strangers in honor of past intimacy, unless the friendship had ended due to an extremely vicious action of some kind.

4. Love of Self and Love of Friends

Here, Aristotle moves into the fascinating domain of the love of one's self. If a friend is like a second self, then we must consider our relation to the *first self*, so to speak. A friend may be defined as one who wishes and does what is good for the other, or wishes that his friend live and be safe for the other's sake. A friend may also be defined as one who chooses to spend time with another and who shares and enjoys the same things. Both of these defining characteristics of friendship can be seen most of all in the love of mothers for their children, and indeed, all of these characteristics are found in the relationship of a good man to himself.

A virtuous person is at one with himself in desiring with his whole soul the things that are truly good for him *in accordance with his intellectual nature, wherein lies a man's true self.* Such a good person delights in his own company, because he has pleasant memories of his past and hopes of a joyful future, and because his studies have supplied him topics worthy of contemplation. He is sympathetic to his own thoughts, desires, pleasures, and pains, since he knows them most intimately. Such a virtuous person, then, relates in the same way to his friend, for his friend is a *second self.*

Friendship such as this is not possible among vicious people because they are at war with themselves, either through lack of self-control which causes them to seek, not what is truly best, but what is pleasant (though harmful), or through cowardice or laziness, in which they shirk the difficult but good duties they know they ought to perform. In cases of extreme wickedness, those who commit heinous crimes through moral depravity may come to hate themselves so much that they end their lives in suicide. Note, also, how poorly-behaved people seem to always seek out company and avoid being alone, so they do not have to remember and dwell on the bad things they have done. Having no lovable characteristics within them, they love not even themselves. Their souls are divided, and they often come to regret the illicit pleasures they have sought. This is a miserable state we would do well to avoid. *Only if we strive to be virtuous can we be friends with ourselves and, thereby, also friends with others.*

5. Goodwill and Friendship

Moving on to different things that seem to be like friendships or components of friendship, Aristotle starts with feelings of goodwill. Goodwill resembles friendship, but is not the same thing, because it can arise in an instant and for people we do not know, without their ever knowing it. Neither does it involve the intensity and desire that accompany feelings of friendship. Still, goodwill can be seen as the beginning of friendship, just as the pleasure we feel at looking at someone can be the seed of erotic passion. No one loves who has not enjoyed the sight of the beloved, and yet just because a person finds another attractive does not mean that person loves him unless he longs for him when absent.

Goodwill, then, can be seen as an unproductive or inactive friendship, for friendship requires that we *act* on our good wishes for our friends. Only among virtuous people, as they grow accustomed to one another through their interactions over time, may the seed of goodwill blossom into true friendship. We should note, as well, that in general *goodwill emerges as a result of virtue and goodness,* whenever one finds another person to be excellent in some way, as we see even in the case of spectators who feel goodwill towards excellent athletes.

6. Concord and Friendship

Concord or harmony also seems to be a characteristic of friendship. This is not merely being in agreement on some issue, since even people who don't know each other may hold the same belief. Neither is it agreement about anything, such as matters of astronomy; *concord is agreement about issues that involve a common good.* A city, for example, is in concord when its people agree that office should be elective, that an alliance should be struck with the Spartans, or that Pittacus should rule them if he is willing.[8] When people all want to rule or want the same things for themselves as the characters in Aristophanes' play *Phoenissae* do, they are in conflict rather than concord.

Concord, then, can rightly be seen as political friendship, because it concerns things of common interest that impact people's lives. Such harmonious agreement is found in good people. They are in concord with themselves and with others because their desires are consistent and constant, not battered about like opposing currents of a strait in the sea, and they desire what is just and advantageous, not only for themselves, but for the common good. Among base people, concord is not found, or is found only to a minor extent, for they seek to obtain their own good while failing to do their share in service to the common good. They spend time compelling others to do what is just, but do not do it themselves.

7. Beneficence and Friendship

Benefactors seem to better love their beneficiaries than the latter love them in return, and sometimes people explain this in terms of credit and debt, for the creditor wants his debtor to remain safe so he can repay him, while the debtor wishes the creditor did not even exist! This is not adequate to explain the beneficence of true friendship, though, because *benefactors love the friends they have aided even if they can never be of use to them.* We see this kind of love displayed by a craftsman for his product, for he loves the work of his hands more than that work would love him were it to acquire a soul and come alive! And perhaps this love is most extreme in the case of poets who so dearly like their own poems that they dote on them as if they were their own children. It is much the same for the benefactor, for the beneficiary is, in a way, the benefactor's product and he likes it more than the product likes the producer.

---

8. Pittacus was elected to rule Mytilene on the island of Lesbos in the 6th century BC. When he stepped down after ten years, the concord was ended because he no longer desired to rule.

Giving benefits actualizes our natures as human beings, for we exist to live and to act, and we love the recipients of our gifts because we love to express our being through actions. A maker loves his handiwork, then, because a maker by nature loves his own being and *the potentiality within his being is expressed in living actuality by what he has produced.* Further, when a person produces something noble, the nobility lasts, while what is only useful eventually passes away. Finally, we also tend to love best what has taken effort to achieve; for example, self-made people are fonder of their wealth than those who have inherited it. Similarly, receiving a gift may take no effort while giving one may require hard work. Indeed, this is why mothers love their children more than fathers do, in light of the suffering they undergo bringing their children into the world, together with the fact that they better know that the children are theirs. This applies to other benefactors as well.

8. Self-love versus Selfishness

It is debatable whether or not a person should love himself most. We criticize as shameful and call "self-lovers" those who seek everything for their own sakes, while we praise those who act out of honor and act for their friend's sake over their own. And yet we love most the friend who loves his friend for his own sake, wishing the best for him even if no one else knows about it, and this is our attitude to our own self. It is from this attitude that friendship can branch out to others, by treating a friend as a second self. As the proverbs relate, "friends are of one soul," "friends share alike," "friendship is equality," and "friends are nearer to the knee than shin," for all of these describe a man's relation to himself. Each of these views of self-love is right to a certain extent.

Those who are criticized as "self-lovers" are those who seek the greatest share of things like riches, honors, and pleasures for themselves, because they consider them the best things and matters of competition. These people seek to gratify the appetites and desires of the lower, animal parts of the soul and are rightly chastised for the baseness of their behavior.

We do not criticize, however, the person who strives above all to act justly, through self-control, and in accordance only with virtue.

This sort of person actually awards himself with the greatest of rewards, because he gratifies his rational intellect, the highest controlling aspect of the soul, through acting voluntarily only for what is noble and excellent. This person most truly loves himself, because this part of the soul truly defines what we are as human beings. *Therefore, the man who truly loves himself will busy himself with praiseworthy actions, and if every person had this kind of self-love the world would overflow with deeds for the common good.*

The virtuous person should love himself, but the wicked person should not, because the latter will harm his neighbor for seeking the kinds of goods that he seeks, following passion rather than right reason. The wicked man's actions conflict with what he ought to do, while the good man ought to do as he does, because the intellect chooses the best course, and the good man obeys his intellect. Indeed, because the good man chooses the right and the noble above all else, there may be times when *the good man may sacrifice his wealth or even his life for his friends,* when this is the most noble and praiseworthy course. *At times he may even forgo a noble act himself, when by doing so he allows his friend to do it and the friend to attain the honor.* In sum, then, *a person should be a lover of self, but not in the way that most men are.*

9. Why a Happy Person Needs Friends

Some have argued that happy people are self-sufficient and have no need of friends, as is expressed in the saying, "If the gods bless us with good fortune, what need of friends?"[9] This perspective sees friends in terms of their *usefulness,* rather than as second selves pursuing virtue together. Aristotle had established in book 1 that happiness is not merely an end state, but an ongoing activity, and it reaches its heights in the contemplation of one's existence and of excellence and virtue. Hence, *when a man has virtuous friends, he can contemplate and relish not only his own being and virtuous acts, but that of his friends, each a second self to him.* Indeed, as the poet Theognis of Megara once wrote, *the society of good men is a training*

---

9. Euripides, *Orestes,* v. 667.

ground in virtue. Therefore, to truly be happy, a person needs virtuous friends.

10. How Many Friends Do We Need?

Should we seek as many friends as possible or follow the advice given for hospitality "to have neither many guests nor none?"[10] Aristotle sides with Hesiod and notes that we can have too many friendships of all three kinds. As for friendships of utility, who would want to spend all his time paying back favors received from a vast number? For friendships of pleasure, a few seem to be enough, just as a little seasoning is all that food requires. And even for virtuous friendships, too few or too many both present problems, as a city could not be formed of merely ten people, and one of a hundred thousand citizens would no longer be a city. There must be a limit in the number of real friends each of us may have, and this must be determined by the number we can live with and share time with. Further, those in a circle of friends should also be friends with one another, a hard thing to manage in great numbers. Further still, the *intimacy* of close friendship, like that of love, is not found in groups of people, but *in twos,* as has been celebrated in song through the ages. The person who is friends with everyone is, in a sense, friend to no one, except perhaps as a fellow citizen. We should be happy to obtain even a few virtuous friends.

11. Friends for Better and for Worse

Friends need each other in ill-fortune for assistance and in good fortune to enjoy benefits together. In bad times, a virtuous man may decide not to seek out his friend in order to spare the friend the pain of seeing his distress. Still, we should go and seek out our friends in their times of need, even if they do not ask, for that is the noble thing to do, as it is to seek them out when fortune has blessed

---

10. From Hesiod's *Works and Days,* 715. A modern translation, with flair, of this verse and the next: "Don't get a reputation either as Mr. Popular or The Misanthrope, or as someone who hangs out with low-lifes, or who always bad-mouths everyone better." *Hesiod: Theogony, Works and Days,* C. S. Morrissey, trans. (Vancouver, BC: Talonbooks, 2012), 109.

them, since *it is nobler to rejoice in the benefits of another than to seek them out for oneself. In short, friendships are always desirable.*

12. What Friends Do Together

There is nothing lovers enjoy as much as the sight of each other, and so, too, do friends cherish the chance to see and spend time with each other. Friends form a community of close companionship, and we stand in relation to our friends as we do to ourselves. Therefore, whatever kinds of activities fulfill us, we seek to pursue them in the company of our friends. This is why we find drinking buddies, dice-playing friends, athletic training partners, teammates, those who hunt in pairs or small groups, and those who philosophize together. Friendships enhance whatever we choose to do, which is why the friendship of base people is vicious, since it facilitates base pursuits, while the friendships of good people are virtuous, as they grow in virtue whenever the friends pursue noble activities together. "So much then, for friendship," writes Aristotle.

2

Aristotle's Matchless Legacy of *Philia* and *Arête*

He draws a conclusion concerning the good, that friendship between virtuous men is good and is always increased in goodness by exemplary conversation. Friends become better by working together and loving each other. For one receives from the other an example of virtuous work which is at the same time pleasing to him. Hence it is proverbial that man adopts noble deeds from noble men.

⌐St. Thomas Aquinas, *Commentary on Aristotle's Nicomachean Ethics*[1]

The Benefits of Friendly Philosophic Conversation

ST. THOMAS AQUINAS found Aristotle's *Nicomachean Ethics* of such importance that he produced his own commentary on every single line, and further incorporated much of the books on friendship into his own masterwork, the *Summa Theologica*. One conclusion we might draw from Thomas's explication, above, of the last chapters of the *Nicomachean Ethic's* book nine is that Aristotle himself may be among the world's most stellar examples of the benefits noble men receive from philosophical discussion with other noble men.

Aristotle's achievements have undoubtedly been stellar. In social scientist Charles Murray's *Human Accomplishment: The Pursuit of Excellence in the Arts and Sciences, 800 B.C. to 1950,*[2] his statistical

---

1. St. Thomas Aquinas, *Commentary on Aristotle's Nicomachean Ethics*, C.L. Litzinger, O.P., trans. (Notre Dame, IN: Dumb Ox Press, 1993), 587.
2. Harper Collins Publishers, 2003.

analyses measuring the extent to which great achievers influenced others found Aristotle to be the most influential thinker in world history in the realm of the arts and sciences, ranking first in philosophy and second only to Darwin in biology.[3] Narrowing the field from human accomplishment as a whole to human friendship in particular, Aristotle again appears as the most foundational thinker. In the most up-to-date treatise on friendship that I came across, modern philosopher Alexander Nehamas writes in his first chapter, "Aristotelian Foundations," that Aristotle's "influence has been immense," and that "the philosophical tradition is overwhelmingly on Aristotle's side" in terms of fundamentals like the "unalloyed good" of friendship and the three kinds of friendship Aristotle described.[4] This is not to say the Nehamas himself and other thinkers have not differed with some of Aristotle's conclusions. His conclusions, however, are too important and influential to just be ignored.

So, while Aristotle's own legacy has been indeed been immense, to say the least, we should also make note of the legacy that Aristotle himself had inherited from his teacher of nearly twenty years, Plato, who, in turn, had been taught by Socrates. Before Aristotle wrote about friendship in the *Nicomachean Ethics,* and most likely before that in chapter 7 of his less fully developed *Eudemian Ethics*, Plato had written an elegant dialogue on the topic, with Socrates himself leading the cast of characters. Modern philosopher Mortimer Adler once wrote: "Plato raised almost all the questions that everyone should face; Aristotle raised them too and, in addition, gave us clearer answers to them."[5] In the case of friendship, I certainly agree.

In Plato's *Lysis,* Socrates converses with a cast of characters that includes some pairs of friends, but his probing questions on the nature of friendship, how it develops, its relationship to kinship and

---

3. The only other thinker to win a gold and silver medal, so to speak, in two separate fields was Sir Isaac Newton, ranking first in physics and second in mathematics.

4. Alexander Nehamas, *On Friendship* (New York: Basic Books, 2016), 12–13.

5. Mortimer J. Adler, *Aristotle for Everybody: Difficult Thought Made Easy* (New York: Bantam Books, 1978), ix–x.

whether or not it is born of human neediness end up with no firm resolutions. Aristotle addresses some of the same issues early on, but he arrives at some conclusions, as we will see shortly.

Aristotle wrote in the first book of the *Nicomachean Ethics* that political science, of which he saw ethics and friendship as parts, does not admit of exact precision in its conclusions and is informed by the opinions and actions of men who are considered wise. Hence, he borrows widely from the writings of great Greek poets and sages such as Homer, Hesiod, Solon, Sophocles and Euripides.

Nicomachean Ethics: Book 8 Commentary

Chapters 1–5: On the Nature of Friendship and Its Three Kinds

Aristotle's *Nicomachean Ethics* is focused on human happiness and the virtues that lead us to it as perfections of our various powers as human beings. Having discussed happiness and various moral and intellectual virtues in the first seven of ten books, Aristotle devotes a good fifth of his book to friendship. He relates in chapter one of book 8 that friendship is necessary for human fulfillment, that it effectively flows forth from virtue, and that it is a truly noble thing. His early emphasis on the desire for friends even among the powerful and otherwise self-sufficient serves to answer the speculations in Plato's *Lysis* that friendship is born from human deficiency and neediness, for the noblest men seek friends whom they might benefit. Friendship, he says, is for the young, the old, and those in their prime of life, since, as we might say today, "two heads are better than one." Two friends working together are better able to think and act than either friend alone. Foreshadowing themes he will later develop, he talks of the friendships within families, among citizens, fellow-travelers, and even, in some sense, among animals.

After explaining that we are attracted to things through love, either because those things are pleasant to us, useful in some way, or because they are good in themselves (or at least *seem* good to us), Aristotle launches into perhaps his most famous and thought-provoking contribution to the understanding of friendship, namely, the classification of three kinds of friendship:

The Four Friendships: From Aristotle to Aquinas

- Friendship of utility (*sumpheron*)
- Friendship of pleasure (*hedon*)
- Friendship of virtue (*arête*)

We all have human friendships based to some extent on utility. We tend to befriend (and be befriended by) those who can be helpful to us, or whom we can aid in some way. Friendships built in school or in the workplace often start at this level. We gravitate towards those who might be able to give us a little help or advice, or perhaps to those to whom we can offer some expertise. This is all fine and good, as far as it goes, but utility is the lowest rung of the ladder of friendship. When taken to an extreme, it may not represent much of a friendship at all. Consider the "user" who values a friend only for what the "friend" can do for him. What happens if the friend is no longer of use to the user? No—true friendship, as an embodiment of the love of charity, is not entirely about personal benefit.

The next step up the ladder is the friendship based on pleasure. Such a friendship says not only, "I value what you can do for me," but, "Your presence is pleasant to me." This may build upon the first level of friendship. Perhaps your friend first helped you learn to play a certain sport, and now you enjoy pursuing and discussing it with him. This tells your friend not only that you value what he has done or can do for you, but that you appreciate something about his person.

At this level of friendship, you acknowledge that there are things in the other's personality or character—perhaps a sense of humor, hopefully an embodiment of some talent or virtue—that make it pleasant for you to be around him. But this level of friendship also has its limits. It still says that you value your friend for what he gives to you; in this case not help, but pleasure. What will happen to your friendship if he ceases to please you (or you cease to please him)?

The third and highest level of friendship is the friendship of virtue. This is the friendship that truly embodies human excellence. The true friend has a love and concern for the welfare of his friend; the focus of this friendship is not on the good one can receive, but on the good that one can give to another. Aristotle notes that "very likely friendships of this kind are rare." His main reason for saying this? "Virtuous men are scarce." You see, in order to have a loving friendship based on one's own virtue and the love of the virtue in another, the friends themselves must be virtuous.

Is not Aristotle's classification of friendship a call to classify our own friendships and our own roles within them? Which of our friendships are friendships of excellence or virtue—those being the only complete, perfect, or true friendships? Have we sought out virtuous friends? Have we worked to acquire the virtues that can make us good friends to others?[6]

Aristotle compares and contrasts the types of friendships in chapter 3 and declares that not only are virtuous friendships *the best*, but, because of the stability of character that virtue brings, also *the most enduring*, as long as the friends continue to express their affection through ongoing interactions.

Chapters 6–8: Important Nuances in the Kinds and the Acts of Friendship

Aristotle next considers the kinds of people who tend to form the different kinds of friendship, noting that old people and those who are by nature more cranky or morose are least likely to form friendships or pleasure or virtue, because they don't enjoy each other's company. They may still wish each other well and help each other when in need, but they do not seek out the familiarity that is necessary for friendship to grow. Certainly it makes sense that more austere, aloof, or surly people will be less inclined to form friendships, but is it not interesting that Aristotle groups the elderly along with them? Does this seem true in our day? Loneliness among the elderly does appear to be prevalent, with many in nursing homes or in homes of their own who lead lives of quiet desperation, especially if many of their old friends have passed away and adult children

---

6. In previous chapters of the *Nicomachean Ethics,* Aristotle described eleven moral virtues of courage, moderation, liberality, magnificence, greatness of soul, ambition, gentleness, friendliness, truthfulness, wittiness, and justice, as well as intellectual virtues of science, understanding, wisdom, art, and prudence, the practical wisdom that lies at the crossroads of both intellectual and moral virtue—prudence being a virtue by which we seek to *know the truth* (in terms of valid means to moral ends) and to *act to achieve moral goods.*

neglect them. Is this typically due to the older person's own surliness or lack of interest in friendship? Did the elderly in 4th century BC Athens tend to be a grumpier lot due to the perennial illness and afflictions that accompany old age without the benefit of our modern medical treatments to assuage their pains and disabilities? These are just some questions to think about. We might also want to consider our own lives, whether or not we find ourselves less interested in forging the bonds of new friendship as the years go by, and to what extent we respond to or seek out the friendship of the elderly.

It appears that, in Aristotle's day as in our own, the young tend to form friendships of pleasure more easily. To adapt a modern song lyric just a bit, "girls (and boys) just want to have fun," and children and teens love to associate with one another in pleasurable pursuits such as games, sports, and the production or enjoyment of music. It is difficult, however, to form enduring friendships with very many, because the nature of true friendship is very intense, like a laser beam that loses its penetrating power if its rays are diffused too widely. True friendship requires a lot of time and effort; it takes a while to learn who is good and worthy of virtuous friendship, and it is easier to be friends with a greater number of people when those relationships are based merely on usefulness or pleasure. Of the two incomplete friendships, the ones based on pleasure are more likely to blossom into true friendship, because true friends will seek to spend their time together and even the virtuous do not seek out what is unpleasant. We might argue, as well, that people who have cultivated characters of excellence will most likely also be most pleasant to spend time with—whining, complaining, insulting, backstabbing, belligerence, indifference, and the like tend to be unpleasant and are not to be found in Aristotle's (or hopefully anyone else's) list of virtues.

In chapter 7 Aristotle covers some interesting nuances regarding relationships wherein the parties hold positions of superior or inferior status, such as father to son, an older person to a younger one, a man toward a woman, and any sort of ruler toward the one he rules.

Now the example of "a man toward a woman" representing a relationship of superior to inferior status is likely to rankle modern readers, and in regards to the *capacities,* or at least the *roles* of women, Aristotle was often in keeping with the traditional views of his day, which were common not only in practice but in the writings of many philosophers.[7] Still, it is reported that Aristotle had such a loving relationship with his wife, who died long before him, that, though he would later have a son by another woman—indeed, the Nicomachas to whom this great work of ethics was mostly likely dedicated[8]—before his death he chose to be buried beside the wife of his youth.

Aristotle poses an odd and intriguing question in chapter 7—that is, whether or not a friend who wishes good things for his friend would will that his friend should become a god. If not, it would seem that a friend does not wish his friend the highest of goods. Aristotle opines, nonetheless, that a friend will *not* wish that his friend would become a god, because friends wish each other goods and gods are self-sufficient, needing no external good, including friendship. Further, a friend wishes his friend goods as another *self,* so the friend must remain the kind of being that he is. We wish goods to others as human beings. I bring this unusual line of reasoning up mainly to plant a seed that we will harvest in the writings of St. Aelred and St. Thomas, who had very different ideas about the potential for friendship between the human and the Divine.

In chapter 8, Aristotle moves toward an intriguing analysis of giving and receiving, of loving and being loved, within the context of friendship. He concludes that friendship is defined more by loving than by being loved; note the consistency with the words Christ reported by St. Paul: "It is more blessed to give than to receive" (Acts 20:35). To prove his point, Aristotle writes of the enjoyment a mother finds in loving, even in cases where she must give her child away. (I find this interesting, as I happen to type away on the Feast

---

7. Some of the ancient Stoics who came after Aristotle would become champions of women's equality in terms of their intellectual capacities and rights as human beings. The Roman Stoic Musonius Rufus (ca. AD 20–100), for example, would argue in his *Lectures* 3 and 4 that women should study philosophy just like men, since they have the same capacity for virtue, and that girls should be educated in virtue just like boys. We will see in Part III of this book what St. Aelred had to say about the equality of men and women.

8. Though Aristotle's father was also named Nicomachas.

of the Immaculate Conception, commemorating the conception of the loving mother who would give her Son away to the world.) Aristotle says much more, but his argument is summed up by his declaration *that loving is the virtue of friends.*

Chapters 9–12: Friendship and Justice in the City and in the Home

In the next chapters Aristotle casts a very wide net over friendship, so wide that what he found relevant to an examination of *philia* might surprise modern readers by its scope. He addresses friendship within associations or communities of all kinds, drawing out the implications of the proverb that "what friends have is in common." The closer the association, the more is held in common. Further, the closer the association, the greater are the demands of justice, since it would be far worse to rob a friend than a fellow citizen or to strike one's father than anybody else. Aristotle notes that smaller associations are often made for the mutual benefit of members with similar interests or life circumstances, such as those among fellow soldiers, religious groups, or dinner club members. Aristotle notes that all sorts of associations are parts of the broader political community, which seeks the good of all and should foster such friendships.

In chapters 10 and 11 Aristotle provides his intriguing analysis of the different political systems of monarchy, aristocracy, and timocracy, their degenerate forms of tyranny, oligarchy, and democracy. That democracy comes last might seem surprising to us, but Aristotle believed that political power should properly rest with people who have significant property at stake, and that democracy is the least degenerate or vicious of the deviations because it differs slightly from the legitimate system of propertied timocracy, in contrast to tyranny, which is the most extreme and worst form of political degeneration. Most relevant to our concerns here, however, is that Aristotle believed that both justice and friendship are impacted in predictable ways by each kind of government, whether in their proper form or when perverted. Also of particular interest are Aristotle's comparisons between monarchy and parent/child relationships, aristocracy and husband/wife relationships, and timocracy and older/younger sibling relationships.

Indeed, his line of thinking in comparing family relations to forms of political organization and leadership calls to mind modern psychological theory, particularly research pioneered by Diana Baumrind in the 1940s on "authoritarian," "authoritative," and "laissez-faire" or "permissive" parenting styles. In general, "authoritative" parents—those who set high standards for their children, hold clear expectations, employ reason when disciplining them and display plenty or warmth and kindness (perhaps as would philosopher-kings)—tend to have children with higher self-esteem and levels of achievement. As Aristotle might have warned, children exposed to the other styles do not fare so well. Children of "authoritarian"-style parents, for example—the most rigid, demanding, punishing, and lacking in warmth—are likely to be moody, anxious, and more prone to be followers than leaders. With Aristotle and Baumrind's ideas, in mind we might ask ourselves what kind of communities we are forming in our own homes and how they might impact our friendships with those within them.

Chapter 12 digs further into these friendships within families, providing a wealth of insights. Note how Aristotle sees parental friendship as the ideal pattern of all friendships. Recall that a friend is "a second self." A child is indeed a part of each parent, the closest possible thing in nature to a "second self." The relationship between siblings builds upon the shared nature of "common blood" and upon the fact that siblings of similar age go through life together— as the proverb Aristotle cites declares, "two of an age get on well together,"[9] having shared similar experiences. Indeed, in any reference to modern research on human psychological development, children and adults of the same age group are often grouped together for analysis because they have similar backgrounds. Members of these age groupings are called "cohorts," after ancient Roman military units who, so to speak, marched through life together. Aristotle does not neglect members of the extended family; we might ask ourselves to what extent we see our cousins and distant relatives

---

9. In Lipzinger's translation of St. Thomas's commentary, the phrase is lyrically rendered: "men of a year like to draw near."

as friends and what we might do to deepen our extant bonds of friendship with these "blood relatives."

Last but not least, Aristotle provides a paean to marital and familial life, positing that the formation of marriages and families is more natural than even the formation of cities. Perhaps he implies that the human being is something more than his famous "political animal"—a "familial animal"—though it is the city and not the family that most clearly distinguishes us from other animals. Husbands and wives provide great benefits and pleasures to each other, including the common good of children, that which holds the man and woman together (or at least that which did so in Aristotle's day and place). Further, the friendship of husband and wife can provide plenty of ground to exercise, develop, and delight in uniquely human virtue, if the husband and wife are virtuous.

We might ponder to what extent the deterioration of two-parent families over the last several decades in America may have hindered the capacity of children to form virtuous friendships. Might the lack of stable models and sharers of virtuous friendship within the home increase the likelihood that children will seek alternative forms of companionship in associations such as gangs, groups seldom lauded for the cultivation of virtue and citizenship?

Chapters 13–14: Why Friendships May Go Awry

Aristotle concludes book eight with an analysis of why things may go wrong in friendships between persons of equal and of unequal status. He notes that friendships of utility are the most prone to quarrels and conflicts because these imperfect friends are most likely to keep what we might term a mental ledger, balancing credits of benefits received and debits of benefits conferred, as they track each other's *quid pro quos*, making sure their mutual back-scratching is performed in equal measure. Aristotle believes that human nature is such that, without the cultivation of virtue, each friend is biased to believe that what he has given away is more valuable than what he has received, and therefore to feel shortchanged by his friend. The virtuous, however, delight in providing benefits to each other and do not quarrel over such things. Such conflicts are even rare in pleasures based on friendship, since it would seem absurd for a friend to complain to his friend that he does not please him adequately, when he is free to spend his time in other people's company.

In disputes within friendships among unequal parties, problems usually arise when the person of superior status feels entitled to receive more than his inferior friend because better benefits are due to better people, while the inferior party believes he is entitled to more because it is the duty of a powerful friend to help a friend in need. Aristotle opines that there is some truth in both opinions: the better friend should receive more *honor,* while the lesser friend should receive more *assistance,* since honor is the proper reward for excellence and beneficence, whereas assistance supplies need. To avoid conflicts in friendships between unequal parties, friends should give one another, not what is of *equal value in worth,* but what is *possible* for each to give. Here, too, Aristotle notes that, while it is impossible for a son to ever fully repay his father for the gift of his life and upbringing, a father almost never disowns his son, unless the son has become exceptionally wicked.

Perhaps this will remind some readers of the poignant story we find in Luke 15:11–32. The prodigal son who had squandered his inheritance believed that he had crossed the final line of wickedness. He came back and told his father "I am no longer worthy to be your son." The father did not ask for equal recompense for his loss, but only for what was possible for his son to give—his act of sincere and humble repentance. Of course, Christians believe that the father of that prodigal son symbolizes a Father with a capital F, the Father of an entire race of prodigal sons and daughters, a Father who never expects equal payment from his children for their existence and for every good that he provides for them. He expects in return only the love that it is possible for them to give.

Nicomachean Ethics: Book 9 Commentary

Chapters 1–3: Continued Analysis of Conflicts between Friends

It is in the first chapter of book 9 that *philia, arête,* and *philosophia* (friendship, virtue, and philosophy) meet in a most interesting way. Aristotle notes that conflicts may arise in friendships when what people receive in return from their friends is not what they expect or desire, which can feel the same as getting nothing. We see such mismatches, for example, in the case of Sophists, who offer wisdom for money but instead provide their clients with, well, *sophistry*—words designed to deceive rather than enlighten. Friends who seek true philosophical wisdom in study and conversation together—the kind of wisdom that defines and fosters truth and virtue—will not be deceived or disappointed in what they offer each other. In fact, so great is the boon of the true philosopher to others that he is like a parent or even a god, whom we can never fully repay for his great favors![10]

In chapter 2, Aristotle considers various situations in which the bonds of friendship should or should not outweigh obligations to others in accord with justice. In chapter 3, he provides a very thoughtful and humane examination of when friendships should or should not be called to a close, and, if they are ended, how one should treat a former friend. In short, the partial friendships of pleasure and utility are ended naturally when one party is no longer pleasant or useful to the other, while friendships of virtue, by nature the most perfect and enduring, are difficult things to end. Such friendships should be ended if one friend has seriously abandoned virtue and become vicious—but even then, a true friend should consider whether his fallen companion is amenable to being helped back up and guided back to virtue. Only when the friend has become incurably vicious, unwilling and unable to return to an upright character, should the friendship be dissolved.

We might also encounter cases wherein one friend grows greatly in virtue and the other stagnates, so that one is like an adult in virtue and the other remains like a child. In such cases, Aristotle says, we may need to allow friendships to dissolve, but we should always maintain a special regard for our former friends, treating them with particular kindness in honor of the bonds we once shared. We might reflect at this point to see if we can call any former friends to mind, perhaps from our childhood or youth. Are there ways that we do show them special care and affection when our paths happen to cross?

10. (So while we're on the subject: Thank you, Aristotle!)

Chapters 4–8: Self-Love and the Love of Friendship

We now come to the heart and soul of Aristotle's conception of virtuous friendship. He proceeds to list defining features of friendship with others, but first notes that these characteristics all derive from how we relate to ourselves—we wish to continue to exist, wish for good things and act to achieve them, take pleasure in our own company, and seek to be of one mind about important things. He then elaborates on five elements of friendship deriving from self-love:

• A friend desires his friend to *be*, to exist.

• A friend desires good things for his friend.

• A friend does good deeds for his friend.

• A friend takes pleasure in his friend's company.

• A friend is of one mind with his friend, rejoicing and sorrowing in almost the same things.

These are five things that virtuous people wish for themselves and for their friends.

The first can be clearly seen in cases of bereavement, in the anguish we experience when a good friend no longer exists. We wish our friends to exist for their own sakes, and when a friend dies, we may feel as though we have lost part of our own self. Indeed, we will see in the next chapter that such an event precipitates Cicero's entire dialogue on friendship.

Though incomplete in itself because it can arise for people we do not even know and lacks the inherent familiarity necessary to the intense love found in friendship, *eunoia* (goodwill), examined in chapter 5, is an element of true friendship and is necessary for the development of new friendships.

When we have goodwill for our friends, we wish for them the same good things we wish for ourselves. In chapter 6, this *homonoia*, a union or likeness in mind and heart, is usually translated as *concord* or *harmony*. Cicero considers this feature of friendship so essential that, while Aristotle's conception of true friendship is commonly called "virtuous friendship," we will refer to Cicero's conception of friendship as "harmonious friendship." There we will explicate more fully what Cicero called "*concordia*."

Of course, if we truly wish good things for our friends, we will take action to try to achieve them. Aristotle examines the exchange of benefits between virtuous friends in chapter 7, noting that beneficence—the giving of benefits or accomplishment of good deeds for our friends—is truly something fine and noble. Further, the giver of benefits therefore feels pleased with the person he has been able to benefit. The friend has afforded him the opportunity to exercise his beneficence. In that sense, the benefactor has also benefited himself.

Speaking of benefits to oneself, Aristotle devotes chapter 8 to what he acknowledges as a puzzling and debatable issue: that of the apparently competing demands of loving oneself and loving others. Should we love ourselves or others more? What are we to make of this notion of *philautia* (self-love)? This remains a great question for modern philosophers (and, I expect, for modern readers too).

In her insightful book-length examination of Aristotle's philosophy of friendship, Suzanne Stern-Gillet examines issues of what Aristotle meant by the self: one's own as distinct from other selves, doing things for the sake of another self, self-love, self-love as it relates to egoism, and self-sufficiency. Commenting on Aristotle's presentation of self-love in book 9, chapter 4, she writes, "Aristotle presents *philautia* as a state of serenity that is enjoyed by virtuous persons who have become true to their own selves."[11]

In her examination of the deficient self-love that Aristotle ascribes to the wicked and the incontinent, she notes an interesting parallel between Aristotle and the prophet Isaiah, who wrote "There is no peace, says the LORD, for the wicked" (Isaiah 48:22).[12]

Stern-Gillet concludes that Aristotle has achieved two things in his analysis of self-love in virtuous friendship:

1. "He has shown how sweet are the rewards of virtue."[13] The person who loves his true self experiences serenity, having internalized moral virtues, and becomes free from the distress of the remorse and regret that come from vicious actions.

11. Suzanne Stern-Gillet, *Aristotle's Philosophy of Friendship* (Albany, NY: State University of New York Press, 1995), 86.
12. Ibid., 96.
13. Ibid., 101.

2. He has made himself ready "for what he viewed as the most sat-
isfying personal relationship of all, i.e., primary friendship."[14]

To reiterate our last chapter's summary of Aristotle's book 9, chapter 8:

> We do not criticize the person who strives above all to act justly,
> through self-control, and in accordance only with virtue. This
> person gives himself the greatest of rewards, because he gratifies
> his rational intellect, the highest controlling aspect of the soul,
> through acting voluntarily only for what is noble and excellent.
> This person most truly loves himself, because this part of the soul
> truly defines what we are as human beings. *Therefore, the man who
> truly loves himself will busy himself with praiseworthy actions, and if
> every person had this kind of self-love the world would overflow with
> deeds for the common good.*

Chapters 9–10: On the Need for Friends and How Many We Need

Aristotle writes that the people who describe those who are blessed
with plenty as self-sufficient and having no needs of friends confuse
the friendship of utility for true friendship of virtue. Indeed, happiness is an ongoing activity in pursuit of virtue and in its contemplation. As Lorraine Smith Pangle, another contemporary philosopher
who has written at book length on Aristotle's theory of friendship,
has observed, "most importantly, having a friend means at bottom
not having a possession but engaging in an activity of the soul."[15]
When a person has a true friend, he can relish not only his own
existence and virtuous acts, but those of his "second self" as well.
We might say that no man is so rich in virtue that he cannot grow
even richer by sharing and growing in virtue with a friend, as they
train each other toward greater heights in fulfillment of their
human potentials.

As glorious it is to have friends, friends of all three types must be
limited in number—recalling that we would not want to spend all
of our time dispensing or receiving favors in friendships of utility,

---

14. Ibid.

15. Lorraine Smith Pangle, *Aristotle and the Philosophy of Friendship* (Cambridge, MA: Cambridge University Press, 2003), 184.

and that, as for friendships of pleasure, a little seasoning is all a dish requires. We will also recall that friendships of virtue are rare simply because virtuous people are rare—though perhaps this suggests a, well, rarefied view of true friendship. We certainly need not be *completely* virtuous to engage in virtuous friendships, but we should at least be dedicated toward growth in virtue.

Aristotle's main point here, however, is that virtuous friendships must be limited because we can only share our time with a limited number of friends. His statement that one hundred thousand citizens would be too many for a city might sound strange to modern ears—indeed, my own relative hamlet of Springfield, Illinois passed that mark decades ago. Yet the kind of *polis* (city) Aristotle had in mind was a city small enough that most citizens would know each other, share the same general concerns, and have opportunities for first-hand involvement in their governance. Ideally, Aristotle implies, our circle of friends will be small enough that our friends will also be friends with each other. Intimacy is essential to friendship for Aristotle, so that the friend to everybody is, in a sense, the friend to nobody. To obtain even a few virtuous friends is a good thing indeed!

Chapters 11–12: On the Joys, Acts, and Benefits of Friendship

Although Aristotle has argued forcibly that true friendship is not based on need, he still seems to endorse our old saying that "a friend in need is a friend indeed." In chapter 11 he posits that friends need each other for better or for worse, so to speak—to enjoy benefits together in good times and to provide support in bad times. He insightfully observes that although, while experiencing hard times, a man may not seek out his friend's company and aid because he does not want to distress his friend, it is noble for a man to seek out a friend that he knows to be in need, even if he does not ask. The presence of friends is always a good thing.

Finally, in chapter 12, Aristotle exults—as much as the Father of Logic is wont to do—in a final paean to the blessings and joys of virtuous friendships. True friends love the very sight of each other and seek to spend time together in all sorts of activities, from drinking to sports and all the way to the Philosopher's own preferred activity of philosophy itself. Such friendships make whatever we do better and, through them, friends also make one another better.

Here, in the last line of chapter 12, Aristotle rather tersely sums up, "So much, then, for friendship." He had to move on to a consideration of pleasure and happiness in his tenth and final book.

More than 2300 years have passed since the death of Aristotle, and yet subsequent writing on friendship—particularly in distinguishing the three kinds of friendship—keeps circling back to old Aristotle again and again and again. In the recent words of Dr. Gregory Sadler, a modern philosopher and philosophical counselor:

> The fact that Facebook and other social media tends to blur together distinct types of relationships might be better seen as simply a reflection of a longstanding confusion about what friendship is and what it means. How longstanding a confusion? It's one going back to the days of the ancient Greeks, and not just back to Aristotle—he rattles off a number of already generations-old puzzles and confusions bearing precisely upon friendship in his own day at the beginning of book eight! It's also a confusion that keeps on arising perennially—and perhaps even perpetually, one is tempted to add.
>
> That's exactly why we keep coming back to Aristotle's distinction, generation after generation, and still finding it useful. I'd like to stress that it is more useful as a set of starting points, however, than as the final word on the issue.[16]

We move now to consider what Cicero had to say about friendship in our third of eight chapters. Rest assured, however, that we are far from hearing the last word from Aristotle on his foundational conception of friendship.

---

16. Gregory Sadler, "How Hard is it to Find an Aristotelian Friend?," *Orexis Dianoetike* blog, https://gbsadler.blogspot.com/2016/12/how-hard-is-it-to-find-aristotelian.html, posted on 12/06/16.

PART II

Marcus Tullius Cicero's Harmonious Friendship

✛

Friendship is of universal concern, and to read such an intelligent man, and such a loyal friend, on this theme one cannot fail to be of value at any place or time. Indeed no one else has ever dealt with the subject in so memorable a fashion.

～Michael Grant, *Cicero: On the Good Life*[1]

---

1. *Cicero: On the Good Life*, Michael Grant, trans. (London: Penguin Books, 1991), 174.

3

Harmonious Friendship
in the *De Amicitia*

For friendship is nothing else than an accord in all things, human and divine, conjoined with mutual goodwill and affection, and I am inclined to think that, with the exception of wisdom, no better thing has been given to man by the immortal gods.

⌒Marcus Tullius Cicero, *On Friendship*[1]

IN THIS CHAPTER I will provide summaries of Cicero's brief book *De Amicitia* (On Friendship), also known as the *Laelius*, or *Laelius on Friendship*, after the main speaker of the dialogue. Though the book is a dialogue on its face, the character of Laelius holds the floor for the vast majority of the text, while his sons-in-law Quintus Mucius Scaevola and Gaius Fannius Strabo mainly provide background information, ask him questions, and prod him to continue to share his thoughts on friendship.

Gauis Laelius Sapiens the Younger (c. 190–after 129 BC) earned the cognomen or nickname *Sapiens*, "the Wise," for both his political and military prowess and his broad philosophical learning. Laelius was known as the close friend of Roman general and twice consul Scipio Africanus Minor, adoptive grandson of Scipio Africanus, the revered military strategist who had defeated Hannibal of Carthage in North Africa (hence his cognomen "Africanus"). The dialogue takes place shortly after this victory and is occasioned by the younger Scipio's somewhat suspicious sudden death in bed in 129 BC.

---

1. Cicero, *On Friendship*, W.A. Falconer, trans. (Cambridge, MA: Harvard University Press, 2001), 131.

Additional context and commentary will come in our next chapter. Here, I will provide summaries of some key points of interest in each of the 27 chapters of *De Amicitia*.[2] In composing these summaries I had access to Cicero's Latin text through the Loeb Classical Library edition from Harvard University Press, as well as three English translations.[3] I will conclude by noting that, as was the case for the summaries of Aristotle's writings on friendship, the subheadings for each of the chapters are not in the original. They are my own contributions, intended to emphasize key concepts and to aid readers in going back and tracking down ideas of interest, either in this text or in the originals. I invite readers to keep their eyes open for familiar themes encountered in Aristotle's work as well as new and unique Ciceronian contributions to our great philosophical legacy on friendship.

1. Setting the Stage with Thoughts on the Loss of a Beloved Friend

Here is the first and the last of the twenty-seven sections of *On Friendship* in which Cicero speaks in his own voice, setting the stage for his elegant, eloquent dialogue on the nature and nurture of friendship. He notes that in his work *De Senectute* (On Old Age), the great Stoic sage Cato the Elder was cast as the speaker, and that, when Cicero read his own work, even he imagined that Cato was talking to him! In a similar vein, in this work "written as a most affectionate friend to a friend on the subject of friendship,"[4] Gaius

---

2. I hope that you will pardon my continued use of the Latin title. Because Cicero, though born in the humble village of Arpinum about 75 miles southeast of Rome, seems the quintessence of Roman language and culture, the usage feels appropriate.

3. *Cicero: On Old Age and Friendship*, Frank Copley, trans. (University of Michigan Press, 1967) as reprinted in *Other Selves: Philosophers on Friendship*, Michael Pakaluk, ed. (Indianapolis, IN: Hackett Publishing Company, 1991); *Cicero: On the Good Life*, Michael Grant, trans. (London: Penguin Books, 1991), and the aforementioned Loeb Edition, *Cicero XX: On Old Age, On Friendship, On Divination*, W. A. Falconer, trans. (Cambridge, MA: Harvard University Press, 2001, first published in 1923).

4. Ibid., 113. (The friend to whom both dialogues were addressed was Atticus.)

Laelius is cast as the main speaker, who has gathered with his sons-in-law after the death of his dear friend Scipio Africanus. Cicero directly requests of his reader: "Please put me out of your mind for a little while and believe that Laelius himself is talking."[5]

Let us honor noble Cicero's request and listen in at this somber gathering of more than two thousand years past, in the days of Republican Rome.

2. Greek and Roman Models of Virtue Praised for Words and Deeds

Laelius's son-in-law Fannius begins by acknowledging that there was no better man than his father-in-law's friend Africanus. He relates that Laelius himself is among the few who, like the astute civil lawyer Lucius Atilius and the courageous statesman and historian Cato the Elder, have been found truly wise among the Romans. Yet he notes that Laelius's wisdom is unique in that he is counted wise not only for his natural endowments and character, but because of his devotion to study and to culture, so that he is considered wise not only in the manner of the ignorant masses, but also by learned men. Indeed, Fannius compares Laelius to Socrates, whom the oracle at Delphi deemed "most wise," and declares that Laelius's wisdom lies in the fact that he considers himself responsible for his own life, regarding human fortune as inferior to virtue.

Laelius thanks Fannius for the kindness of his words, but declares that while he cannot claim the high honor his son-in-law has bestowed on him, Fannius has hardly praised Cato nearly enough. Cato does not suffer even in comparison to the man proclaimed wise by the oracles, for while Socrates is praised for his words, Cato is praised for his deeds!

3. Death is No Misfortune for the Noble Man

Moving next to the heart of the matter—the loss of his friend—Laelius says that he bears no delusion that Scipio has suffered misfortune in his death. If anyone has suffered a loss, it is Laelius himself, yet for a man to display great anguish over the loss of a friend is not

---

5. Ibid.

the act of a man who loves his friend, but of a man who loves himself. Laelius believes that all has gone well for Scipio unless he had planned to live forever. He lived such a good and long life that a few more years would hardly make a difference, and little could have been added to the fullness of his life.

4. Musings on the Immortality of the Soul

Here, Laelius elaborates his belief that bodily death does not imply the death of the soul. The two do not necessarily perish at the same time, and he gives credence to the beliefs of his forefathers who conducted reverential rites for the dead, which they would not have done if they did not believe it made any difference to the deceased. This view was also held by the Pythagorean philosophers of lower Italy, and indeed, while Socrates typically argued for both sides of an argument, he consistently argued that human souls were divine and that at death the path for heaven was laid open to them, the ease of their journey depending upon their virtue in life. Scipio himself spoke in a similar vein, as if from a premonition, just days before his death. Laelius argues that to grieve at the death of Scipio would bespeak more of envy than friendship. Finally, if death is truly the end of all experience, then, while there is nothing good in death, there is nothing evil either, since the state of death would be the same as if Scipio had not been born—and yet Scipio was born, which is a joy to Laelius and to the State!

Laelius is buoyed and pleased by the thought that the memory of his friendship with Scipio will endure, as, indeed, throughout all of history only three or four such pairs of friends are reported.[6] This section concludes with the son-in-laws' request that Laelius share with them his opinions on the nature and practice of friendship.

5. On the Nature and Goodness of Friendship

Laelius begins by agreeing that the subject is a noble one, while arguing that he has no special skills to talk about it off the cuff, as do

---

6. Falconer, page 124, suggests that the pairs Cicero references were Theseus and Pirithous, Achilles and Patroclus, Orestes and Pylades (to be discussed in chapter 7 below), and perhaps Damon and Phintias (or Pythias).

some Greek philosophers who train themselves to speak on the spot. Still, he agrees to make the attempt, and begins by telling his companions that friendship should be placed above all other human things, since nothing so conforms to human nature and is of greater value both in good times and bad. Next, he notes (echoing, but not citing Aristotle) that friendship is possible only among good men. He makes clear that he opposes the doctrine of some Stoic philosophers who say that no man is good unless he is wise, and who argue that no human has completely attained such wisdom. Laelius believes that normal men can become good and wise enough to share in genuine friendship, and therefore he and his sons-in-law will proceed "with their own dull wits," as the saying goes, and ponder the good things of friendship.

Let the philosophers keep their "truly wise" man. Laelius will consider men good who model loyalty, integrity, justice, generosity, who have freed themselves of greed, lustfulness, and insolence, and who have shown unwavering character—men who have followed their true nature and provided for us guides to living the good life.

While nature has built in us the tendency to foster relationships to those near to us—loving countrymen better than foreigners and relatives better than strangers—friendship excels such ties in that goodwill, which may disappear from ordinary relationships, cannot be absent from friendship. Further, while nature has tied us together with so many people in so many kinds of relationships, friendship is so rare and so narrow that its bonds of affection are shared by only two or a few at a time.

6. Friendship Defined

Here Laelius gives us Cicero's definition of friendship, which was used as the quotation at the start of this book's chapter: "*For friendship is nothing else than an accord in all things, human and divine, conjoined with mutual goodwill and affection*, and I am inclined to think that, with the exception of wisdom, no better thing has been given to man by the immortal gods." Wise people value virtue over wealth, health, power, honor, and sensual pleasures, and it is virtue itself that spawns and nourishes friendship, so that, where virtue is lacking, there is no friendship. Further, Lalius tells us, we need no high-flown philosophical analysis to define what we mean by "virtue," or "goodness," for we know what we mean when we use these words in everyday speech, besides the sort of men to whom they are commonly applied, such as Cato, Scipio, and others.

Now among such virtuous men friendship provides such powerful benefits that words can hardly describe them. Indeed, how can a man live what Ennius[7] called "the life worth living" unless it rests upon the mutual benevolence of friends? What is sweeter than having a confidant with whom one may share one's thoughts as easily as though talking to oneself? How could one fully enjoy prosperity without a friend to share it with, or adversity without a friend to bear it with? Friendship makes prosperity glow more brightly and diminishes the burdens of adversity by distributing and sharing it.

7. The Hopefulness, Unity, and Nobility of Friendship

While friendship has many advantages, it surpasses all things in that it projects a bright ray of hope into the future, and it keeps our spirits strong and unfaltering. *A man who looks upon a friend looks upon an image of himself.* Therefore, friends are near though far away, rich when poor, strong when weak, and, stranger still, alive though they have passed away, as a friend holds a dead friend in high esteem with vivid recollections and with poignant longings. This is why deceased friends can be seen as fortunate, and their survivors praiseworthy, for their love. Remove the bonds of friendly benevolence from the universe and no state or household would survive, no fields be tilled. The greatness of the power of harmonious friendship can be seen by what happens when it is replaced by enmity and ill will. For what house is so sturdy, or state so strong, that it cannot be utterly destroyed by hatred and division?[8] And who does not praise a man who shares even great dangers for his friend? In a play recently written by Laelius's friend Marcus Pacuvius, during a scene in which the king asks which of the two friends before him is Orestes so that he might put him to death, the entire theater erupted in applause and rose to their feet when Pylades

---

7. Quintus Ennius (239–169 BC), "The Father of Roman Poetry."
8. Cf. Abraham Lincoln's House Divided speech and Mark 3:24–25.

declared, "I am Orestes!" while Orestes insisted "I am Orestes!"[9] Men by nature approve of such acts of true friendship, even though they may not be able to perform them themselves.

8. How Love Gives Rise to Friendship

Laelius cheerfully complains about how Fannius and Scaevola have compelled him to continue to discourse on friendship and then reveals that he has often pondered the true origins of friendship. Does it lie in weakness and want, so that we seek out friends to supply us with the things that we lack? No—Laelius believes in another cause, more ancient, more beautiful, and springing from nature herself. For it is from love (*amor*) that we derive our word for friendship (*amicitia*), and friendship moves us to goodwill. Advantages may appear in friendship even when it is feigned, but there is no falsehood or pretense in the nature of friendship; it is genuine and spontaneous, and that is why it seems to spring from our nature, which is inclined to love and affection rather than to calculation of advantages we might derive. We see this in animals in the care of their offspring and between children and parents.

We love a person when we see in him habits and character congenial to us, and we look upon him as a shining light of probity and virtue. There is nothing more lovable than virtue. Indeed we feel affection even for people we have never met when we hear of their virtuous deeds, as we hate figures we know from history who are infamous for their vice.

9. How Virtue, Not Gain, Stirs the Souls of Friends

If virtue garners our affection for people we do not know, how much more are our souls stirred by the virtue and goodness of those with whom we come in close contact! Love begets familiarity and care for one another, which further strengthens that love, engendering a marvelous glow of benevolence. Those who attribute friendship to a weakness or lack render it a lowly thing of ignoble birth, a child of

---

9. This play of unknown title was based on the subject matter of Euripides' *Iphigenia in Tauris*. Modern moviegoers may recall a similar scene in which scores of men arise before the Romans, declaring, "I am Spartacus!" "I am Spartacus!" "I am Spartacus!" etc.

inadequacy and poverty. If this were so, then the less capable a man was, the better he would be suited for friendship, whereas the truth is surely the opposite. The more a man pursues wisdom and virtue, becoming sufficient and depending on no one to meet his needs, the more he will seek out and cherish friends.

What, Laelius asks, did Africanus need of him? By Hercules, nothing! And neither did he need Africanus, yet he admired and loved him for his virtue, while Africanus loved him for the virtue he perceived in his character. Surely great advantages came to each of them through their friendship, but it was love, not hope of advantages, that drew them together as friends.

This view is rejected by men, who, like cattle, measure everything merely by the pleasure it provides. They abase themselves by focusing so much on the petty and mean that their thoughts cannot arise to anything as lofty as true friendship of affection and benevolence. The views of the vicious may be dismissed. Men of virtue find pleasure in each other's virtue and derive profit from it likewise, competing in doing honorable favors for one another and thereby spurring each one on to nobler deeds of benevolence. When advantages cease, so, too, do friendships based on advantage. Friendships based on nobility of character derive from unchangeable nature, and therefore endure forever.

10. Challenges to Friendship

Scipio, Laelius tells his sons-in-law, frequently noted that there was nothing harder than to maintain friendships all the way to the end of life, because there were many reasons they might disintegrate. The relationship might cease to be mutually advantageous, opinions like political views might change, and even men's characters might alter due to adversity or through the burdens that accompany old age. He would note, at these times, how the friendships of childhood are often set aside along with the toga of childhood.[10] Further, of

---

10. In a coming of age ceremony at age 15, Roman boys would doff the *toga praetexta* of childhood that featured a broad purple stripe on its border and don the *toga virilis* of manhood, a pure white toga signifying the rights and dignities of an adult male Roman citizen.

those friendships that continue, many are later broken off due to rivalries, perhaps for a wife or for some other good that both could not share. Those that endure yet longer may be ended during a struggle for some political office, for while friendships among base people may end in fights over lust for money, noble men strive for honor, glory, and office, and rivalries for these things may turn close friends into the bitterest enemies.

Another bane to friendship is the serious conflict that arises when a man demands that his friends do something for him that is immoral or illegal. When a man refuses such a request, the friend may charge him with a violation of the rules of friendship, proclaiming that his own asking shows that he would have done the same if he were asked. These sorts of complaints not only destroy friendships, but produce bitter enmities. So many are the ways that friendships can be broken that a man must be both wise and lucky to be able to escape them all.

11. The Love of Friendship Stretched Too Far

Here Laelius asks if there should be limits to the love of friendship and discourses at length on Roman examples of men who persuaded their friends to join them in arms against their countrymen in attempts to gain kingly power, some of whom came to Laelius himself seeking leniency when their plots collapsed around them. Indeed, when Gaius Blossius begged pardon of him for his support of Tiberius Gracchus's revolt, he explained that so great was his respect for Gracchus that he felt he should do whatever he asked of him. Laelius asked Blossius if he would set fire to the Capitol if Gracchus asked him to, to which he replied that Gracchus would never ask such a thing, but if he did, then he would comply. Laelius found this response vicious and insane. He concludes that friendship never justifies sinning on a friend's behalf, since friendships are based on virtue, and deliberate vicious acts destroy the very virtue that friendship is founded upon.

12. A Law for Honor among Friends

Here, then, is a law to be established among all friends: *neither ask dishonorable things of a friend, nor do such things, if asked.* Friendship between men is never an excuse for assaults against the state. This is a very important principle, for illicit assaults against one's country are never attempted unless the instigator is supported by associates. Friendship does not pardon alliances of the wicked.

13. The First Law of Friendship

Laelius then posits this principle in positive terms as the first law of friendship: *Ask of friends only what is honorable, do for friends only what is honorable, and don't even wait to be asked.* Friends should be zealous, eager, and ready to help one another in virtuous ways— including in acts of counsel and advice—with frankness and even with sternness when the situation requires it. Laelius champions such solicitousness and closeness and disapproves of some Greek sages who advise not to get too close to one's friends or, even worse, to form friendships for the protection or other advantages they provide, rather than out of goodwill and love. By that standard, the weakest and most helpless in character would long for friends the most. What a noble philosophy that is! They take the sun from the sky when they remove truly noble friendship from life, for we have no more delightful gift from the gods.

Virtue, that upon which real friendship is based, rejects the loathsome things that oppose it, as when kindness rejects malice, temperance rebuffs lust, and courage defies cowardice. Indeed, those most just are most appalled at injustice, the brave most affronted at cowardice, and the temperate most offended by wantonness. It is the mark of the well-ordered soul to rejoice in the good and to be pained by evil. Therefore, friendship is not to be neglected because of the pains it might bring if a friend becomes dishonorable, any more than we would reject virtue because with it comes awareness of, and sorrow at, evil.

14. Virtue Forges the Bonds of Friendship among Virtuous Men

Virtue joins people in friendship. When a virtuous soul sees virtue in a kindred spirit he is drawn to the other in love. How absurd it is to be attracted to so many lifeless things like public honors, glory, a house, fancy clothing and adornments and the like and to take little delight in other human souls capable of virtue and of love. Nothing gives more pleasure than the return of our benevolence toward another and the sharing of interests and services for one another. Further, nothing attracts us towards friends more than a likeness of character. By nature good men are attracted to one another, and nature seeks out that which is like itself. Nature thus endows good men with kindly feelings toward one another, and some degree of goodness is found as well in the common, ordinary man. Virtue is not without feeling or excessively exclusive. It binds together entire nations for mutual protection and the common good.

Those, then, who say that personal advantage is the basis of friendship take from friendship its most charming link. It is the friend's love alone that gives us pure delight, and any advantages we receive become pleasurable only because we know that they derive from his loving zeal in providing us service. Indeed, the greatest friendships are not cultivated among the most needy, but among those most blessed with wealth, power, and most especially virtue. It is a good thing, however, when friends are, at times, in need. Laelius himself is thankful that he was able to display his zeal and affection for Scipio when Scipio came to him seeking counsel. No, friendship does not arise from advantage, but advantage does flow from friendship.

15. Fortune's Fools Do Not Know Friendship

We will not learn of friendship from those who exalt luxury and pleasure, for they know nothing of friendship through learning or through living. For who is there, in the name of gods and men, who chooses unlimited wealth and every material good, but has no person to love and to share it with him? Tyrants live this way. They are feared by men and live their lives racked by suspicions and anxieties. People pretend to care for them while they maintain power, but if they fall, as they usually do, they learn in an instant how poor they are in friends. King Tarquin[11] reported that it was when he was sent

11. Lucius Tarquinius Superbus, a legendary ruler reported to have died in 495 BC, was the seventh and final Roman king. After overthrowing him the Roman people declared that they would never have another king. Interestingly, when the

off into exile that he learned which were his true friends and which were false, when he no longer had power to reward or punish them. Yet, because of this king's haughty arrogance, Laelius doubts that he could have had any true friends at all. For not only is Fortune blind, she produces blindness in those whom she embraces, and what is harder to bear than Fortune's fools? How many likeable men take on airs and spurn old friends when they are raised in rank, power, or wealth? How foolish can they be? They procure for themselves all manner of things that money can buy—horses, slaves, fine clothing, costly furniture and the like—but they do not procure friends, life's best and most beautiful furnishings. Indeed, they often procure these material things for the benefit of the stronger whom may later prey upon them, but even if they should have the good fortune to hold onto them, they do not bring happiness if they are not shared with friends.

16. Improper Guides to Friendship

Laelius takes issue with three *erroneous* principles of friendship:

1. We should feel toward our friends the same way we feel toward ourselves.

2. Our goodwill and good deeds toward our friends should precisely match their goodwill and good deeds toward us.

3. A should value his friend just as he values himself.

Indeed, he believes that these three views, though widely held, sell friendship short.

The first, he says, is simply untrue, because a man should do hard things or forgo good things for the sake of his friend that he would not perform or suffer for his own sake. The second view reduces friendship to a petty accounting of credits and debts, as though it were merely a business transaction. True friendship is so rich and affluent that a friend does not fear that the superabundance of what

---

Roman republic gave way at the end of Cicero's life span, the new rulers would claim, not the title of king, but of *Imperator*, a title the Romans gave to military generals. Many kings of other nations would soon be ruled by leaders bearing this title, rendered in English as *Emperor*.

he gives may spill over on the ground, or that more than his rightful measure may flow toward his friend. Worst is the third view—that a person should value his friend as himself—because sometimes people become discouraged and hold themselves in little esteem, yet they should always esteem their friends and provide them with encouragement, instilling hope and optimism in their souls.

Yet some have proposed a principle even more inimical to friendship; Scipio himself used to condemn it most vociferously. This is the notion—perhaps falsely ascribed to Bias, one of the ancient Seven Sages of Greece—that we should love our friends as if someday we would hate them. How selfish and petty to tally up our friend's misdeeds, and perhaps even encourage them, so that one day, if needed, they might serve as ammunition against him! This is truly a principle destructive to friendship. We should never begin to form a friendship with the kind of person we could come to hate, and Scipio thought that, even when unwise friendships have been formed, we must endure much from our friends and not lightly break from them.

17. Choosing Friends Wisely

We should observe, then, these proper limits and guides to friendship:

> 1. We must choose friends of blameless character.
>
> 2. Then there must be complete harmony in all things without exception, even if the aims of the friend are not entirely commendable, but involve matters of life, death, or reputation, and would not result in complete disgrace.

Scipio would often speak of how painstaking the choice of one's friends should be and yet how carelessly friendships are usually formed, for men who could tell you how many goats they owned could not tell you how many friends they had. We should seek out trustworthy and loyal friends, but this is not easy, since such men are rare. A wise man will be careful of the direction of his goodwill and the speed with which he befriends others, as he would, when driving a chariot with a new team of horses, test the character of the horses now and then. It is particularly difficult to form friendships with those involved in politics and public office, for rare is the man who will put his friend's chance for advancement ahead of his own.

While Ennius may be correct that "a friend in need is a friend indeed," there are two ways in which most men are found to be fickle and disloyal; the first way is when men who become successful abandon old friends they no longer need, and the second way is when men abandon a friend who has come across hard times. Those individuals who remain unshakable and firm in their friendships despite their own prosperity or their friend's calamities are truly rare—in fact, they are almost divine.

18. Foundations of Friendship: Trustworthiness, Loyalty, and Friendliness Too

The foundation of steadfast loyalty among friends is trust, for nothing lasts that cannot be trusted. We must choose for a friend a man who is honest, forthright, and sociable, with interests similar to our own. We cannot trust a person of deceitful character with many twists and turns, and those who do not share our aims will not make for reliable friends. Our friends should neither delight in making malicious charges against us nor believe such charges when they are made by others. This illustrates, again, what Laelius has said from the start—that friendship is possible only between good men. Good men observe these two rules: 1) never to be deceptive or hypocritical, and 2) neither to believe malicious charges against a friend nor even to entertain a suspicion that they could be true. Friends, too, should be friendly—that is, affable and graceful in speech and manner toward one another—which adds no mean seasoning to friendship. While there is merit in seriousness and gravity, friendship should be sweeter and more relaxed, more inclined in all respects to courtesy and pleasantness.

19. New Friends vs. Old Friends: Which Ones Win?

While the formation of new friendships is good, we must not prefer them to old friendships, for friendship, like wine, improves with age. We prefer things that are familiar, even horses or inanimate objects such as landscapes. There is truth to the saying that men must eat many pecks of salt together before a full friendship is formed. We should not shun the buds and green shoots of new friendships, which hold promise of bearing fruit, but we should always reserve a special place for old friendships, for nothing matches the power of customs built over time.

It is most important for friendship that superior and inferior friends should stand on equal footing. Scipio, for example, was a highly eminent man in Laelius's circle, and yet he never put on airs of superiority to any one of them. Indeed, Scipio even treated his brother Quintus Maximus—a renowned man, but nowhere near his equal—as his superior because his brother was older than him. Scipio went out of his way to elevate the dignity of all of his friends and relatives, something that each one of us should imitate. Whether we are endowed with a superior intellect, virtuous character, or great fortune, we must share their benefits with friends and family in the hopes of increasing their dignity thereby. This feeling should be strongest of all for our parents: "For the fruit of genius, of virtue, and indeed, of every excellence, imparts its sweetest flavor when bestowed on those nearest and dearest to us."[12]

20. How Unequal Friends Should Behave

Superior individuals should put themselves on the same level as friends and relatives who are their inferiors, and those who are inferior should not protest that others exceed them in genius, fortune, or dignity. Alas, there are many such inferior individuals who complain about their betters, and even about the favors they provide for them, especially if they claim to have done something difficult for their superior out of a sense of duty or love. Such services should be kept in mind by their recipients and never mentioned by those who bestow them. Some people make friendships unpleasant because they constantly believe that they are slighted. These people truly feel inferior, and a friend must do what he can, in words and actions, to help them cast off their sense of inferiority.

We must provide aid to our friends within the limits of our powers to bestow it, but also within the limits of our friends to bear such aid, because some men will be unable to bear the burdens of certain

---

12. *De Amicitia*, Faulkner translation, 181.

honors and offices. We must choose friends wisely and care for them dearly, but we should not let our affection for them prevent them from doing important things that they must do. For example, if a friend has to part from us for some time for important duties, it is a sign of weakness and selfishness to become overly emotional and, by our grief, hinder our friend in his actions. Such behavior is weak, effeminate, unreasonable, and unbefitting of friendship. We must consider with care both what we demand of our friends and what we permit them to demand of us.

21. Breaking Up is Hard to Do

Calamities of a sort do occur, at times, in the breaking up of friendships. If one's friend acts viciously toward oneself or others, the friendship may need to be broken. Ideally, as Cato once said, it should be gradually unraveled rather than suddenly cut off. In cases of extreme viciousness, however, the break may need to be immediate, with no further affection or contact. When lesser problems arise, such as a change in character or in political opinions among friends, the friends must be sure to not to give the appearance of transforming into enemies, for there is nothing more disgraceful and unseemly than to go to war with one with whom you shared an intimate relationship. Scipio once broke with Metellus because he had deceived his friend Laelius in gaining an office he sought by pretending that he was not in the running, but Scipio made the break without fostering bitterness or resentment. When severe discord does arise between friends, the fires of friendship should appear to have burned themselves out "rather than to have been stamped out."[13]

The best tactic to defend ourselves against such ills and injuries is to be careful not to bestow our friendship upon those unworthy of it. Alas, worthy men are rare, for everything excellent is rare, and nothing is harder to find in any realm than a perfect specimen. Most men seek goodness in what brings them profit, treating men as if they were cattle, and lavishing their care on those whom they think will reward them most highly. They do not learn the great les-

---

13. Falconer, 187.

son of the loveliest reward that comes from real friendship, for every person loves himself not for the profit he expects from himself, but because by nature every person is dear to himself on his own account. Unless this same love is carried over to friends, a real friend will never be found, for a friend is as a second self. The man who recognizes this, loves himself, and seeks out another whose soul may so intermingle with his own, has virtually made one soul out of two!

22. Be a Good Person First—and Then Seek Out Another One

Most people—wrong-headedly, and, indeed, shamelessly—expect their friend to be the kind of person they cannot be and demand of their friends what they themselves do not provide. But the right way to begin is to first of all *be* a good person, and then to seek out another person like oneself. Those who do this will form lasting friendships as together they learn to control the passions that enslave most men and to delight in equity and justice. They will learn to stand by each other and will refrain from asking anything dishonorable from one another. They will come to love, cherish, and revere each other in mutual respect. How wrong are those who use friendships to open the doors to vice and sin, for nature has supplied us with friendship as a handmaid to virtue, not an assistant to vice. While virtue alone cannot bring us to the pinnacle of life, it can do so when conjoined in union with a friend. Virtuous friendships provide the richest of blessings that nature has to offer. Such friendships contain within them all that is noble and worthy of pursuit—honor, glory, tranquility, and joy. This is why Laelius repeats yet again the maxim that we must choose our friends wisely, appraising their fitness for friendship before loving them, rather than first loving them and only afterwards appraising their characters. There is wisdom in the old proverb that warns us against arguing the case *after* the verdict is made.

23. The One Thing All Men Deem Worthy

Careful choice of friends is of utmost importance, because friendship is the one thing all men deem worthwhile, even though some of them despise virtue itself, thinking it merely a pretense and an empty display. Some men despise riches, thinking them superfluous, and some feel the same way about office and honors—indeed, some consider strivings for public acclaim as the pettiest of desires. The same difference of opinion holds for all sorts of things, but not for friendship. Here we find men of business, public service, intellectuals, and pleasure-seekers all of one accord, thinking that life without friendship is life hardly worth living. Friendship wriggles its way into virtually every person's life and adds meaning to it. Even if the gods should take us into heaven and display all the glories of the universe, what joy would such a sight bring without another soul to share it with?

24. The Essential Importance of Truthfulness between Friends

As ardently sought as friendship is, it brings experiences varied and complex, and not all of them pleasant. At times a friend must admonish a friend or even reprimand him when he departs from virtue, and we should not be hypersensitive to such correction ourselves. Laelius's friend, the poet Terrence, spoke the truth when he stated in his *Andria*: "Indulgence wins friends, but truth earns ill will."[14] Still, while truth can be troublesome, complaisance and flattery are worse, for they allow one's friend to rush headlong toward ruin. We must admonish with carefulness, frankness, and tact, so that our advice is firm, but not harsh, and our admonitions are not scoldings. Some men are too sensitive to bear even such gentle counsel from their friends, and there is little hope for them. Cato used to say that some men profit more from the bitter words of their enemies than from the sweet words of their smiling friends, because their enemies often speak the truth, while flatterers never do. How ridiculous, too, that the people who cannot accept honest admonishment are more offended by the fact they have been admonished for wrongdoing than by the fact that they have done wrong.

25. To One's Second Self be True

In sum, it is a part of true friendship to deliver frank but courteous correction and receive the same without resentment, and there is no

---

14. *Andria*, 1, 1, 41: "*obesquium amicos, veritas odium parit.*"

greater danger to true friendship than false and fawning flattery. Such hypocrisy is bad in all circumstances because it takes away one's power to judge what is true, but it is particularly repugnant to friendship, since it destroys the sincerity that friendship is based upon. How can two souls become as one if the soul in one man is always false, fickle, changing in form?

26. Beware Stealthy Sycophants

Laelius elaborates on the perils that flattery and sycophancy hold for true friendship. He warns that the man who most readily falls prey to flatterers is the man who is most satisfied with himself. It is true, Laelius admits, that Virtue loves herself, for she understands her own loveliness. Yet he refers not to true virtue here, but to those who seek a reputation of being virtuous. There are many who would far prefer to be thought virtuous than to actually possess virtue. Now, only fools are taken in by flagrant, open flattery, but there are stealthy men who are crafty in their flattery, pretending at times to disagree and then to acquiesce as if the flattered party has won them over by his greater insight. Still, such unfortunate topics have drawn Laelius away from his primary objective—that of discussing true, harmonious friendships and not the frivolous kind.

27. The Undying Love of Friendship

Returning to true friendship, Laelius once again addresses Gaius Fannius and Quintus Mucius by name, assuring them that virtue both forms and holds together the bonds of true friendship. Virtue itself is complete harmony, permanent and faithful. When she rises to full height and shines forth her true light, she recognizes that light in another, moves toward it, receives its illumination, and a new loving friendship is enkindled by the flames, for both love and friendship are derived from the verb meaning "to love."[15] To love means nothing but to cherish the object of one's affection with no thought of personal advantage, though advantages inevitably flow from true friendships, whether or not they are sought.

The joys of friendship are felt more strongly between peers of the

15. *Amor* is "love" and *amicitia* "friendship."

same age, but Laelius himself has enjoyed important friendships with older men in his youth and with younger men like Gaius and Quintus, with whom he is speaking now. Due to the fragility and instability of human life, we should ever be on the lookout for new friends whom we might love and be loved by in return, for if charity and benevolence are removed from life, every joy flees with them.

Laelius declares that though his dear friend Scipio was suddenly taken from him, he still lives and always will, because the love that his virtue inspired is still alive and will continue to shine its light even on men yet unborn. His memory will provide the courage and inspiration for the accomplishment of great deeds in men's lives. Laelius considers the greatest blessing in his life the friendship that he found in Scipio. They travelled together on military campaigns and on vacations in the countryside. They learned and studied together, secluded from the world in their shared leisure. Scipio's loss might be unendurable were it not for the fact that these memories survive, but even if they were lost, Laelius could still go on in his bereavement, since he is nearing the end of his life and any trial can be endured if it does not last long. Here is how Laelius concludes:

> This is all that I had to say about friendship; but I exhort you both so to esteem virtue (without which friendship cannot exist), that, excepting virtue, you will think nothing more excellent than friendship.[16]

16. *De Amicitia*, 27:104, Faulkner translation, 211.

4

Cicero's Lasting Legacy of *Amicitia* and *Concordia*

Certainly no other author of ancient or modern times has discussed the subject of friendship with so much completeness and charm as Cicero discusses it in his Laelius.

~W. A. Falconer[1]

The Origins of *De Amicitia*

TWENTIETH-CENTURY English translator W. A. Falconer notes that *De Amicitia* is dated to 44 BC, based on evidence including Cicero's own catalog of his books to date in his *On Divination* and a letter Cicero wrote to his friend Titus Pomonius Atticus (110–32 BC) on November 5, 44 BC. In this letter, Cicero asks Atticus when Fannius was tribune, which suggests that he was fine-tuning the *De Amicitia* at the time. *De Amicitia* itself is addressed to Atticus; Cicero declares in the second person "You, Atticus…" as he sets the stage for his dialogue in the first chapter.

Cicero certainly had prior influences in his philosophy of friendship. He was known as a great orator and statesman, and indeed, when he was consul in 62 BC, he was hailed by Marcus Cato as "*pater patriae*" (father of the fatherland) after taking abrupt and drastic action, including the execution of two co-conspirators, to end Cataline's attempted overthrow of the Roman republic. Cicero was a matchless orator in his roles as lawyer and statesman. Philosophy was more of an avocation to him for most of his life, and he was

---

1. Falconer, 106.

better known for Latinizing and promoting Greek philosophy among the Romans, especially the philosophies of Plato and the Stoics as presented in the writings of their more recent successors, than for his own unique contributions. Still, while covering some similar themes, Cicero does not cite Plato's *Lysis* or Aristotle's *Nicomachean Ethics* in his *De Amicitia,* and it has been reported in the writings of Aulus Gellius (c. 125–180) that his greatest influence from earlier Greek writings on friendship may have come via a lost treatise on friendship by Theophrastus, Aristotle's immediate successor at his Lyceum. Falconer points out that in chapter 17, section 62—when Laelius comments that people can tell you the number of goats they have, but not the number of friends—Cicero has actually placed the words of Socrates in Xenophon's *Memorabilia* ii. 4.4 in Laelius's mouth! Nonetheless, Cicero provides plenty of original, and, as Falconer notes, charming, material of his own in the *De Amicitia.*

Chapters 1–2: Preliminary Thoughts on the Wisdoms of Greece and Rome

Aristotle, the philosopher, wrote quite a bit about the political dimensions of friendship in the world of classical Greece. Cicero, the politician, philosophized quite a bit about the friendships he experienced in the highest stratum of republican Roman politics. In Cicero we see an intriguing balance between, and mastery of, both the contemplative and the active life, of speculative and practical reason. At the risk of oversimplifying things, the Greeks were seen as "thinkers" and the Romans as "doers" in Cicero's day. Cicero saw the value in informing Roman political doing by Grecian philosophical thinking, hence his desire to popularize Greek philosophical writings. He set himself to the daunting task of translating Greek philosophical terms into the Latin language and strove, not only to educate fellow Romans in philosophy and virtue, but to inspire them to pursue it. We see this in his use not merely of *logic* within his dialogue on friendship, but of lively *rhetoric* with elegant language and dramatic flair. We see this friendly interplay of Greek and Roman thought—the exchange between thinking and acting—made explicit in the words of Laelius at the end of chapter 2. While

Laelius honors the Athenian Socrates for his great wisdom, he honors the Roman Cato even more, for while Socrates was honored for his *words*, Cato was honored for his *deeds*.

Chapters 3–4: The Immortality of Friendship—and of the Human Soul?

The dialogue of the *De Amicitia* itself is precipitated by the recent death of Laelius's friend Scipio, and when Laelius's sons-in-law question him about how he is holding up to the loss, he launches into a discourse on what a friend's death means, both to the friend who has died and to the friend who survives him. While Laelius is not completely unmoved by the death of Scipio, as some of the most strident Stoic philosophers might advise him to be, neither is he anguished. He knows that death was not a bad thing for Scipio himself, since either his great virtue and merit has earned him an eternal place in heaven, or his soul is no more and unable to suffer pain, depending on which school of philosophers is correct on the matter. Laelius leans toward the former view, held by the Pythagoreans and Socrates.

In a charming statement recalling Aristotle's observation that a friend delights in his friend's very existence, Laelius notes that if death really is the end of the soul, then Scipio is no worse off than had he not been born—and yet what a joy to Laelius, and even to the state, that he was indeed born! How charming, too, is Laelius's declaration that if Scipio is actually enjoying eternal bliss, it would make more sense to *envy* him than to *mourn* him! Further, Laelius takes solace in his expectation that their friendship will live on in human memory, as he recalls only three or four famous pairs of friends recorded in history. Of course, through the *De Amicitia* itself, the friendship of Scipio and Laelius does live on to this day. Would it not be a worthwhile goal for us to establish friendships that would be cherished in the memories at least of a few, and at least for a little while? Perhaps Fannius and Scaevola thought much the same, for chapter 4 ends with both of them prodding Laelius to explain friendship to them.

Chapters 5–9: On the Nature and Nobility of Harmonious Friendship

Laelius humbly declares that to spontaneously discourse on such a topic is more a job for a Greek philosopher than for such an unqualified man as himself. He agrees with the philosophers that friendship is only possible among good men—the virtuous—and yet he criticizes the notion, held by some of the Greek philosophers, that no one is truly good unless he is perfectly wise—and no one is perfectly wise.[2] This implies that friendship is beyond our capability, but Laelius believes that real and practical men, though imperfect in virtue and wisdom, can achieve real friendship. His concerns are not with fancies of speculation, but with the stuff of daily life. Men who, in their actions, display loyalty, honesty, fairness, generosity, and the like are truly virtuous men of good character and therefore capable of friendship.

And what is the nature of the friendship that they share? Here, in chapter 6, Cicero provides his definition: "*Friendship may be defined as a complete identity of feeling about all things in heaven and earth: an identity which is strengthened by mutual goodwill and affection.*"[3] He then declares that it is the best of all gifts of the gods but for wisdom. Note here the emphasis on the accord or "complete identity" of feeling about all things of heaven and earth. Here we see "one soul in two breasts," and that defining harmony of friendship is made strong by *benevolentia* (goodwill) and *caritate* (affection or love). How intriguing to find such lofty thoughts and tender sentiments within the minds and the hearts of the some of the greatest statesmen and generals who ruled the civilized Roman world of their day!

In chapter 6 and the following chapters, Laelius waxes eloquent on the magnificent benefits of such harmonious friendship among ordinary men engaged in daily life, which makes prosperity grow all the brighter and lessens burdens of adversity by dividing and shar-

---

2. Some, such as the Stoics, as we saw earlier, considered Socrates the closest thing to the truly wise man, though Socrates believed that his wisdom lay only in his understanding that he knew so little!

3. Grant's translation, op. cit., 187. Italics added for emphasis.

ing them.[4] He describes the nobility of friendship, the hope that it buttresses within us, the way that it holds households, cities, and indeed, the universe together in harmony. Contrary to Socrates' suggestions in the *Lysis* (though Cicero does not mention them explicitly), Laelius strongly opposes the idea that true friendship is born of a lack or neediness, but argues rather that it springs forth from our inborn inclination toward the excellence of virtue. Virtue itself was a topic dear to Cicero and was the subject matter of his very well-received book *De Officiis* (On Duties), written in under a month in his last year of life, 44 BC, the same year in which he wrote the *De Amicitia.*

Chapters 10–21: Threats to True Friendship and How to Overcome Them

To summarize much in just a few words, Cicero treated next of the various reasons why maintaining friendships through to the end of life is no easy thing to do. Threats to the bonds of friendship include the development of rivalries between friends, changes in political affiliations, and, perhaps most seriously, changes in character, an issue we saw that Aristotle had also addressed.[5]

A particularly dangerous threat involving a change in a friend's character is found when a friend would come to ask another to do some immoral act for him. Laelius states quite clearly that *we should make it a rule not to ask anything immoral of a friend, and that if a friend should ask us for such a thing, we should turn him down.* In chapter 13 he offers, as a first law of friendship, the positive and pro-active equivalent that *we should ask friends only what is honorable, do for them only what is honorable, and do that without even waiting to be asked.* (Those who recall our summary of chapter 17 might note some inconsistency here, and we will address that very soon.)

Cicero provides yet another paean to virtue in chapter 14, noting that it is goodness of character, and not mere hope of personal gain, that attracts true friends to each other. He argues in chapter 15 that

---

4. In the words of philosopher Francis Bacon (1561–1626) in his own *Of Friendship,* "it redoubleth joys and cutteth grief in halves."

5. *Nicomachean Ethics,* book 9, chapter 3.

those who are the most blest are those who most often seek out true friendships, "life's best and fairest furniture." Chapter 16 provides three common misconceptions regarding friendship, as follows:

1. We should feel toward our friends the same way we feel toward ourselves.

2. Our goodwill and good deeds toward our friends should precisely match their goodwill and good deeds toward us.

3. A person should value his friend just as he values himself.

Laelius believes that these widely-held views sell friendship short, for a man should feel *better* about his friend that he does about himself, should strive to *exceed* his friend in goodwill and conferring benefits, and should value his friend *more* than himself. Truly these are no mean feats, and are not the stuff of lukewarm or faint-hearted friendships! Worst of all, you will recall, did Laelius consider the maxim that we should treat our friends as if they would someday be our enemies, a view he considered vile and completely inimical to the harmony and benevolence of true friendship.

In chapter 17, we find an apparent and perhaps real contradiction of Cicero's "first law of friendship" from chapters 13 and 14, which prohibits friends from asking of or doing for the other any actions that are immoral. When he lays out the limits of friendship in chapter 17, he notes, to recap:

1. We must choose friends of blameless character.

2. Then there must be complete harmony in all things without exception, *even if the aims of the friend are not entirely commendable,* but involve matters of life, death, or reputation, and would not result in complete disgrace. (Italics not in original.)

In his second statement, Cicero seems to violate his first law of friendship—though one might suppose, given the previous statement declaring that the character of one's friend should be blameless, that a request for an action opposed to virtue would be unlikely, unless the friend had a change in character or faced a most unusual circumstance. Even here, Cicero qualifies his statement by saying that such an action would be not *entirely* honorable—suggesting some positive merit to the action—and that it must involve a very serious issue and not lead to utter disgrace, since even the bonds of harmonious friendship have limits prescribed by virtue.

In chapter 18, Laelius lays out some traits and behaviors that are musts for lasting friendship. Friends must be trustworthy and loyal. They must never make up charges against each other or believe such charges when they are made up by others. Besides such steadfast dedication to one's friends, friends should also be—well, friendly. Friendship is sweetened by a sense of ease and relaxation in the presence of one's friend. It is made pleasurable by gracious speech, humor, lightheartedness and courtesy.

In Chapter 19 Laelius shows how the loyalty of friendship should endure by noting that while we should not fail to nurture the buds of new friendships, we owe special deference to friends of long standing, having enjoyed the fruits of their friendship over time. Cicero, like Aristotle before him, addresses the issue of friendships between persons of unequal status, merit, or virtue, but Cicero makes it especially personal when his words come from the mouth of Laelius, who proclaims himself as the clearly inferior party in his friendship with Scipio and praises Scipio for never treating him as if he were not his equal. A true measure of friendship, and of concern for others in general, is our behavior toward those over whom we have superiority or authority. As Christians, we might ask ourselves: do we "lord it over" others in inferior positions, or do we treat them with dignity, recognizing that all of us live and move and have our being under one and the same Lord? Last but not least, Laelius sets out a point in chapter 19 that St. Thomas Aquinas will later drive home: we should share our benefits most with those who are nearest and dearest to us, especially our parents.

Laelius further addresses unequal friendships in chapter 20. In keeping with his position and with the political structure of republican Rome, Laelius opines that superior men should be careful that their friends do not feel slighted and should strive to lift them up and assist them, but that they should not promote them into positions that exceed their capacities. Scripture tells us, "Do not lift a weight beyond your strength" (Sirach 13:2). Laelius advises, in essence, that while we should try to strengthen our friends, we should be careful not to lay crushing weights upon them.

Chapters 21–27: Friendship Lived in Daily Life

In chapter 21, Laelius addresses the possibility that friendships may need to be ended, advising that they should be allowed to quietly fade away if possible, since there is nothing more discreditable than that to go to war with one with whom one once was intimate.[6] The best advice for avoiding such breakups is to choose one's friends wisely in the first place, seeking persons of good character worthy of becoming one's "second self." In chapter 22 Laelius notes that before one seeks a *second self* of good character, one must seek to build good character in *oneself*. In declamations with a distinct Aristotelian ring, he tells us that the man fit to seek out a friend is a man who has learned to control his passions and to seek out equity and justice—a man who, in essence, loves what is best in himself, that which makes him fully human. When he respects himself, he may then respect others, allowing him to build virtuous friendships that yield unmatched bounties of peace and joy. As Laelius declares in chapter 23, while some men disdain even virtue itself, thinking its display false and pretentious,[7] all men agree that friendship is valuable.

Part of the value of friendships is that friends share the truth with one another, even when telling the truth may not be pleasant. Laelius addresses these important issues in chapters 24, 25, and 26. The potential for flattery and outright sycophancy was apparently especially great in the day of republican Rome among political friends who wielded great power and who could potentially confer great benefits upon their friends, or upon those who feigned to be friends. Laelius notes that men most prone to flattery tend to be men who are most pleased with themselves. They love to hear others repeat what they think of themselves.

6. Though Cicero does not mention male-female friendships in his text, his last line here calls to mind the phenomenon of divorce, where intimate love may turn to hate. Cicero did, in fact, divorce Terentia, his wife of over 40 years, in the declining years of his life, marrying a young woman whom he soon divorced in turn when she seemed to show no sorrow at the death of his beloved daughter Tullia, who died while giving birth to a child.

7. We might interpret this with a Freudian twist, suggesting the projection onto others of a lack of honest virtue.

This topic was clearly an important one in the last days of Republican Rome in the 1st century BC, as well as in the early centuries of the Roman Empire. The biographer Plutarch (AD 45–120), who included a biography of Cicero within his famous *Parallel Lives*, also wrote a lengthy moral essay entitled *How to Tell a Flatterer from a Friend*, in which he expounds at length on many issues addressed by Cicero.

One such issue was that of the stealthy sycophant who might, for example, pretend to heartily disagree with his companion, and only later pretend to be won over by his superior wisdom.

For those who might enjoy a masterful and humorous depiction of the supremely smooth and stealthy sycophant, I direct my readers to Henryk Stienkiewicz's historical novel *Quo Vadis* for its portrayal of Gaius Petronius Arbiter (AD 27–66), the *arbiter elegantarium* or the ultimate fashion critic of his day. Petronius plied his sycophantic trade most notably upon the erratic young Emperor Nero, at times trying to subtly dissuade him from his excesses—but by so over-inflating his ego that his flattery served to goad him, over time, to ever more absurd displays of his presumably godlike poetic and musical powers, as well as to acts of cruelty. Petronius is believed to have been the author of the widely-read farce *The Satyricon,* which may have revealed his true thoughts about Nero in the person of his most wealthy and vulgar character, Trimalcho.[8]

Interestingly, also among the closest courtiers of Nero was a most notable ancient Roman philosopher, the Stoic Lucius Annaeus Seneca (4 BC–65 AD). Seneca, well aware of the writings of Cicero, himself posited some interesting thoughts on friendship in 124 letters to his young friend Lucilius. We will examine several of Seneca's ideas after commenting on Cicero's final chapter.

In the 27th and final chapter of *De Amicitia,* Laelius returns to the consideration of true friendships between good men. Addressing his sons-in-law Fannius and Mucius by name, he reiterates the essential role of virtue in beginning and sustaining friendships. He notes, too, the essential role of love, declaring that both *amor* (love) and

---

8. I must mention that Leo Genn played a wonderful Petronius in the 1951 film version of *Quo Vadis.*

amicitia (friendship) come from the word meaning "to love," and that to love means to cherish another for his own sake without thought of personal gain. Though gains do indeed flow from friendship, they are a by-product and not its cause. He discusses the closeness of friendships with peers of our own age, but also the goodness of forming friends with those older or younger than ourselves, as he has formed friendships with his two sons-in-law. Indeed, he encourages them to seek new friendships throughout life, because life is transient, old friends may die, and charity and benevolence are what give joy to life. Yet he returns, at the end of his observations, to his reflection upon the loss of his dearest friend Scipio. Even that friendship has not been extinguished completely with his death; Scipio's memory lives on in Laelius and in many others as a spur toward virtue and friendship. Laelius concludes by reminding his friends to remember that nothing is more excellent than virtue and friendship.

The Legacy of *De Amicitia* in the
Palace, the Monastery, and the World at Large

Although Seneca was born less than forty years after Cicero's death, he lived in a very different Roman world. Cicero, a staunch defender of republican government, died at the end of the Roman Republic and the dawn of Imperial Rome at the hands of its first emperor. Young Octavian, later known as Augustus Caesar, was the adopted son of the recently-murdered Julius Caesar. He eventually acquiesced to the demands of his colleague Mark Antony, Julius Caesar's friend, and sent soldiers out to return to Rome with the severed hands and head of Marcus Tullius Cicero, the man who had dared to write and speak out against the tyranny of Mark Antony.

Seneca would come to be the adviser and mentor of a man far crueler than Augustus or Mark Antony—the young emperor Nero, who ascended to rule at the age of only seventeen. The period when Seneca advised Nero was described by the later emperor Trajan as a "golden age," but Nero later shook free from Seneca's advice and adopted a course of such tyrannical rule that by the age of thirty he ordered his own slave to run him through with a sword before he could be captured and killed by being beaten with clubs, the prescribed penalty for Roman tyrants. Before Nero died, he had caught wind of a conspiracy for his overthrow in which Seneca was named as one of the conspirators, and perhaps as his replacement as emperor. Nero ordered his old mentor to take his own life, which Seneca did by opening his veins in a hot bath.

It is intriguing that two of the greatest Latin writers of the end of the republic and the beginning of the empire died through the acts of young, but powerful men who had ostensibly been their friends. Still, both Cicero and Seneca enjoyed true friendships in their lives, despite different political circumstances in their lifetimes. In two of Seneca's famous letters to Lucilius, he advises his young friend in issues of friendship touched on by Aristotle and Cicero, most particularly the final chapter of Cicero's *On Friendship*.

In letter 9, Seneca considers why a man who is self-sufficient would still desire to have friendships, summarizing three key points:

1. Seneca posits, like a good Stoic, that a self-sufficient person does not *need* friendships, but nonetheless *desires* them. He supplies the graphic example of the loss of a limb, or even of one's eyes, through war or accident. Surely a wise man would prefer to have all his parts, but will still seek all the happiness available to him with the parts of him that remain. When such a man loses a friend, he bears the loss with composure.

2. Seneca agrees with the position put forward by Aristotle and Cicero, contrary to Socrates' suggestion in Plato's *Lysis*, that *friendships are not born of need, but rather of a superabundance of virtue*. Here, he explicitly contradicts a saying of Epicurus to the effect that we seek friends to stay by us when we are ill and to help us when we are in need. Seneca proclaims, rather, that *we seek friends in order to have someone to sit by when sick and to help when in need*.

3. Virtue concerns only that which is within our control, and not the happenstance of fortune. Therefore, the man who builds friendships based on *virtue*, rather than the *desire for gain*, is immune to the chance happenstance of fortune, and in that sense he remains self-sufficient.

Seneca, often referred to as a "silver-tongued" orator, is known for the *bon mots* that enrich his writings. One such phrase appears in letter 9, when Seneca advises Lucilius to replace lost friends with new ones. He offers a phrase that the Stoic philosopher Hecato of Rhodes (c. 100 BC), declared to be as potent as any witch's love potion: "*If you would be loved, love.*"

Letter 63 is suffused with both poignant and buoyant thoughts on the loss of friends and the acquisition of new ones. Seneca expresses his regrets at the loss of Lucilius's friend Flaccus, but advises him not to grieve more than is fitting. Consolations on loss were a common literary genre in Seneca's day and formed the basis of some of his own complete essays, including his *Consolation to Marcia*, a wealthy woman who had mourned the loss of her deceased son for a full three years. In letter 63, Seneca warned that excessive, prolonged mourning tends to be a selfish act through which we parade our grief to others and perhaps strive to convince ourselves how much we cared for a lost friend. Because we do not know when our friends may be taken from us, we should cherish them with relish while we have them. In advice that might seem callous, Seneca counsels Lucilius, rather than weeping for the loss of his friend, to seek out a new friend to replace him. He notes that while fortune may have robbed us of an old friend, we rob ourselves of every new friend that we do not strive to make, declaring that a person who cannot love more than one friend probably did not have much love even to offer that friend.

Citing Roman tradition which decreed that women should not mourn for more than one year, Seneca writes that no such rules have been set down for men, because for men any mourning at all is not considered honorable. Yet he admits to Lucilius that he himself was overcome by grief and wept excessive tears at the loss of his friend Annaeus Serenus. The reason for this, Seneca says, was that he had never thought that Serenus, who was much younger than he was, might die first. We would be wise to think of our friend's mortality as well as of our own, as any day could be his last—or ours.

In the centuries after his death, Cicero's writings had a powerful impact on many influential Romans besides Seneca, including Pliny the Elder (AD 23–79), Quintilian the grammarian (AD 35–100), and

Emperor Constantine's adviser Lactantius (c. 240–320). They also held significance for the four original Latin Doctors of the Catholic Church. St. Ambrose (AD c. 340–397) wrote a book, *On the Duties of Ministers,* which was influenced by Cicero's *De Officiis* and included a section on friendship. St. Jerome (AD 347–420) reported a dream he had after his conversion in which an angel whipped him for being more a Ciceronian than a Christian. St. Augustine (AD 354–430) wrote that before he converted to Christianity, it was Cicero's lost work the *Ad Hortensius* that won him over to philosophy. In the next century, Pope St. Gregory the Great (c. 540–604) sought to suppress the writings of Cicero because they were distracting men from studying the Scriptures!

References to Cicero were spotty and often secondhand for the next several centuries, though reportedly the *De Amicitia* was among the most popular of his works, along with his essay on old age. Theologian Peter Abelard (1079–1142) eventually renewed interest in Cicero, but the theologian who most embraced *De Amicitia,* resurrecting it in a Christianized form from within medieval monasteries, was Aelred of Rievaulx (1110–1167), the subject of our next two chapters. Prominent open admirers of Cicero's works over the centuries also included St. Albert the Great (c. 1200–1280), St. Thomas Aquinas (1225–1274), Dante Alighieri (1265–1321), Petrarch (1304–1374), and American Founding Fathers (and "Mothers") including George Washington, John, Abigail, and John Quincy Adams, Thomas Jefferson, and James Wilson.[9]

It is to be hoped that the legacy of Cicero's ideas, especially those espoused in the *De Amicitia,* may also prove valuable to us in our day. With that thought in mind, we move next from the ancient Roman forum 1385 miles to the northwest and eleven centuries forward in time to the medieval English monastery of Rievaulx, where the writings on friendship of Marcus Tullius Cicero, a man who died before Christ was born, became thoroughly and beautifully Christianized by a remarkable but remarkably little-known man, the former chief steward to King David I of Scotland.

---

9. In Carl J. Richard's *The Founders and the Classics: Greece, Rome, and the American Enlightenment* (Cambridge, MA: Harvard University Press, 1994), Cicero's name appears in more than one-fourth of the book's 242 pages.

PART III

St. Aelred of Rievaulx's Spiritual Friendship

The ideas I had gathered from Cicero's treatise on friendship kept recurring to my mind, and I was astonished that they no longer had for me their wonted savor. For now nothing that had not been sweetened by the honey of the most sweet name of Jesus, nothing which had not been seasoned with the salt of Sacred Scripture, drew my affection so entirely to itself.

〜 St. Aelred of Rievaulx, *Spiritual Friendship*[1]

---

1. Aelred of Rievaulx, *Spiritual Friendship*, Mary Eugenia Laker SSND, trans. (Kalamazoo, Michigan, 1977), 46.

5

Spiritual Friendship
in *Spiritual Friendship*

Here we are, you and I, and I hope a third, Christ, is in our midst.
~St. Aelred of Rievaulx, *Spiritual Friendship*[1]

MORE THAN eleven centuries separated the death of Cicero in 43
BC and the birth of Aelred of Rievaulx in AD 1110—a greater time
span than that which separates us from Aelred. Yet the Roman
statesman's influence on the English abbot was vast. Aelred built
upon Cicero's insights on friendship and patterned the topics in his
three dialogues after Cicero's plan, addressing the nature and origins of friendship, its benefits and limits, and its practical difficulties, incorporating approximately one-third of the text of *De
Amicitia* into his *Spirituali Amicitia* (Spiritual Friendship). While
Cicero's writing is clearly the basis of Aelred's dialogue, however, the
Spiritual Friendship ascends to heights unforeseen by Cicero in its
Christian adaptation and transformation.

Despite the elegance of style in Cicero's *De Amicitia*, there is not
much true dialogue—Laelius dominates the conversation in what is
almost a monologue. In Aelred's *Spiritual Friendship*, it is as if we
are eavesdropping on a true dialogue between friends who are ear-
nestly discerning just what friendship is. It is friendship in action,
experienced, and brought to life in text. Readers not fluent in Latin
will need to resort to one of the modern English translations for a

---

1. Ibid., 51.

complete sense of the flow of the conversations within the dialogues.[2] I have tried to convey some of this flow by identifying the speakers, but have written my summaries in the third person.

The scene of the first dialogue is likely the Cistercian abbey at Wardon in Bedfordshire, England, a daughter-house of the monastery at Rievaulx. As its abbot, Aelred would visit Rievaulx at least yearly, and the young monk Ivo with whom he converses in the dialogue has been identified as a monk of Wardon, a friend of Aelred's youth. This first dialogue was likely written within the first ten years of Aelred's tenure as abbot (c. 1147–1157), while the second and third dialogues were likely written within the last years before his death on January 12, 1167. The second and third dialogues take place at Rievaulx some years after Ivo's death. Now joining Aelred are Walter (most likely Aelred's biographer Walter Daniel) and an unidentified monk named Gratian.

I will conclude this brief introduction by noting that, as was the case for the summaries of Aristotle's and Cicero's writings on friendship, the subheadings in this chapter are not in the original text, but are intended as an aid to readers. Again, I invite readers to keep their eyes open for familiar themes encountered in Aristotle's and Cicero's works, as well as new and uniquely Aelredian contributions to our great philosophical (and later, Christian theological) legacy of friendship.

Prologue: A Guide to Chaste and Holy Love

Aelred begins by noting that in his school years, as he was absorbed in various loves and friendships, he was conflicted and drawn toward

---

2. The three English translations at my disposal were Aelred of Rievaulx, *Spiritual Friendship*, Mary Eugenia Laker SSND, trans. (Kalamazoo, Michigan, 1977), St. Aelred of Rievaulx, *Spiritual Friendship*, Lawrence C. Braceland, trans., Marsha L. Dutton, ed. (Trappist, KY: Cistercian Publications, 2010), and Aelred of Rievaulx, *Spiritual Friendship*, Mark F. Williams, trans. (Chicago, IL: University of Scranton Press, 2002, first published in 1994). I found all three translations very helpful, with Sister Laker's language being the most old-fashioned, but also the most lyrical—to my ears, at least.

vice as well as love. This he considers not unusual among youths who do not know the meaning of true friendship. Upon obtaining a copy of Cicero's *On Friendship,* he was captivated by the depth of its wisdom and the elegance of its style. It provided for him a tool with which to gauge his own friendships.

God later led him to a monastery, and there he so grew to love Sacred Scripture that all worldly learning seemed lackluster in comparison. While he often thought of Cicero's writings on friendship, they lacked the "sweet honey" of Jesus's name and the "salt" of the Holy Scriptures.

After a time, however, he considered that Cicero's ideas might be supported by Scripture and the writings of the saints, whereupon he decided to write his own book on the chaste and holy love of spiritual friendship. This he would do in three books, the first on the nature and cause of friendship, the second on its fruits when mature, and the third on how and with whom enduring bonds of friendship may be formed. He concludes by imploring any who might profit by its reading to thank God and to ask Christ to give its author mercy for his sins. If they should find the work unworthy, he asks that they pardon him, since in writing his book he was also obliged to be occupied with many other tasks that come with his position.[3]

Book I: On the Origin of the Species of Friendship

(1–10): On Christian Friendship

Aelred's first words in this dialogue, spoken to his friend Ivo, are as follows: "Here we are, you and I, and I hope a third, Christ, is in our midst." He invites his friend to open his heart to him, since they have the time, privacy, and leisure. He noticed just a while ago, in a lively discussion among the monks on the Scriptures, vices, and virtues, that Ivo remained silent, though at times he seemed to incline his head as if to speak, or would leave the group for a while and

---

3. Would that I could provide such a disclaimer, but this was the first book I wrote in its entirety while retired. Nonetheless, prayers to Christ for mercy for this author's sins would also be much appreciated!

return looking discouraged. From this Aelred deduced that Ivo wanted to speak to him alone.

Ivo responds that he was absolutely correct, and that he appreciated Aelred's concern for him, his "son." Aelred's correct discernment was no doubt produced through the workings of the Holy Spirit in him. Ivo asks permission to have Aelred all to himself in order to open up his heart to him. *Aelred* encourages him to speak freely, since he has observed that Ivo does not prattle on about frivolous things, but he talks about things necessary for spiritual progress. He tells him to prepare to "both learn and teach, give and receive, pour out and drink in," to which Ivo humbly responds that he will be the one who learns, receives and drinks in, since he is young, inexperienced, and under religious obligation to his abbot. *Ivo* then says that he would like Aelred to teach him about spiritual friendship, its nature, value, source, and goals, whether it is open to everyone, and if not, to whom; how it may be preserved in tranquility and brought to holy completion.

Aelred asks why Ivo would seek him out on this topic, since so many ancient sages have addressed it and Ivo has studied such writings, including Cicero's *On Friendship,* in which the ancient thinker expounds in a delightful manner on all of these issues and provides guidelines and precepts for implementing them in friendships. *Ivo* answers that he has studied and enjoyed Cicero's treatise, but (echoing Aelred's own sentiments of the Prologue), declares that because it lacks the "sweet name of Christ" and "the salt of heavenly books," it no longer delights or enlightens him. Still, as a Christian, he would like to see how the many rational things Cicero have said about friendship square with the authority of divine Scripture. More specifically, he seeks to understand how friendship begins, endures, and bears fruit according to the Spirit of Christ.

Aelred replies that he has been won over, but demurs regarding his capacity to *teach* Ivo, pledging rather to *discuss* such things with him. He declares that it is the most sublime and important of themes to speak of how friendship begins, continues, and is perfected in Christ, and asks Ivo what topic he would like to pursue first. *Ivo* responds by asking Aelred to first define the term by describing the precise nature of the friendship that they will consider, "so as not to appear to be painting in emptiness"[4] as they pursue their discussion.

(11–24): The Definition and Nature of Friendship

Aelred responds by quoting Tullius:[5] *"Friendship is mutual harmony in affairs human and divine coupled with benevolence and charity."* *Ivo* agrees that this is a good starting point. *Aelred* summarizes that people who share the same opinion and the same will in human and divine matters, along with benevolence and charity, have achieved perfect friendship. *Ivo* responds that he is not sure what Cicero, a pagan, meant by the words "charity," and "benevolence." *Aelred* replies that perhaps by "charity" Cicero refers to *affection of the heart*, and by "benevolence" the translation of such affections into *deeds*. He notes, playing on a Latin connection to the word *caritas* (charity), that such affection and deeds should be *carus* (precious) to all men.

Ivo is satisfied with the definition, but wonders how it would not apply just as well to pagans, Jews, and even to bad Christians, for he does not believe true friendship is possible without Christ. *Aelred* notes that as they go along they will examine the benefits and limits of that perhaps imperfect definition. *Ivo* says he hopes he will not prove annoying if he agrees to proceed as suggested if Aelred first reveals to him the meaning of the word "friendship" itself.

Aelred repeats the etymological linkage of Cicero, which declares that the word *amicitia* (friendship) derives from the word *amor* (love).[6] He cites his own work, *The Mirror of Charity*, in which he described love as an affection of the rational soul whereby it actively

---

4. Per Laker's translation, 53, "painting on a void" per Braceland, 57, or "painting in thin air" per Williams, 31 if you prefer—a charming touch regardless of translation.

5. Marcus Tullius Cicero. Medieval authors, including St. Thomas Aquinas, often referred to Cicero as Tullius. The translation above is Laker's, 53. Cicero's definition is found in the sixth chapter of *De Amicitia*. The translation we provided in chapter 1 of this book was as follows: *"For friendship is nothing else than an accord in all things, human and divine, conjoined with mutual goodwill and affection,"* following Falconer, 131.

6. *De Amicitia*, ch. 8.

seeks to possess and enjoy the object of affection, and, having attained it though love, enjoys it sweetly, embraces, and preserves it. He notes further that a friend is "a guardian of love" or a guard of the spirit itself.[7] A friend, then, is either the guardian of the friends' mutual love or of his own friend's spirit, wherein he preserves all its secrets and endures its imperfections, rejoicing when his friend rejoices, weeping with him in his sorrows,[8] and feeling with empathy whatever his friend feels.

Friendship, then, is the virtue that binds spirits in sweet love as many become one. Indeed, philosophers have ranked friendship among the eternal virtues, and King Solomon himself would appear to agree with them when he says, "A friend loves at all times."[9] True friendship is therefore eternal, and friendships that end were not truly friendships at all.

Ivo responds by asking why we read of the closest of friends who go on to become bitter enemies. *Aelred* tells him that they will address that issue in due course,[10] but meanwhile to consider that anyone who has tasted the delights of true friendship, though his friend cease to love him, or though he be accused unjustly, injured, tortured by fire, or even crucified, will still love his friend, for again "a friend loves at all times." St. Jerome, too, has made this clear: "A friendship which can cease to be was never true friendship."[11]

(25–30): Exemplars of Christian Friendship

Ivo declares that with such perfection required in friendship, it is no surprise that Tullius said that there are barely three or four pairs of friends extolled in history, and that if the same is true in their time of Christianity, he despairs of ever achieving something of such terrible sublimity. *Aelred* responds with the saying that "*Effort in great things is itself great.*"[12] Indeed, the virtuous mind will ponder sub-

---

7. Here referring to St. Isidore of Seville's *Etymologies,* 10, 5.
8. Cf. Rom. 12:15.
9. Prov. 17:17.
10. In a very detailed discussion starting in Book 3, section 39.
11. St. Jerome, *Letters,* 3:6.
12. Cf. Julius Pomerius's *The Contemplative Life,* 1, Prologue, 2, taken from Pseudo-Seneca's *Monita,* 97.

lime and noble things to understand them more clearly and to acquire knowledge about what should be desired. Therefore, it is an advancement in one's knowledge of virtue when one learns how far from virtue one is.

Still, the Christian should not despair of attaining virtue, since the divine Christ himself spoke in the Gospel: "Ask, and you will receive…"[13] It is no surprise that few pagans pursued virtue because they did not know the Lord and Dispenser of virtue, of whom it is written: "The LORD of hosts, he is the King of glory!"[14] Rather than three or four illustrious pairs of friendships among the pagans, thousands of such Christian pairs could be cited. While Pylades's willingness to offer his life for his friend Orestes was considered marvelous by the ancients, thousands of Christian martyrs have given their lives for their brothers and sisters! Consider Tullius's definition of friendship and those of whom it is written: "Now the company of those who believed were of one heart and soul, and no one said that any of the things which he possessed was his own, but they had everything in common."[15] How could they not be in complete agreement in all things human and divine, since they shared but one heart and soul? How many martyrs suffered tortures and gave their lives for their brethren? Aelred relates the story of a girl of Antioch[16] and the friend who followed her into a house of prostitution to guard her chastity, later sharing martyrdom with her. He relates that he could cite many other such stories, but that he does not wish to be verbose, and is silenced, so to speak, by the vastness of their number; after all, Christ spoke of their coming, and that they would be multiplied beyond counting.[17] Christ also declared, "Greater love has no man than this, that a man lay down his life for his friends."[18]

13. Matthew 7:7, John 16:24.
14. Psalms 24 [23]:10.
15. Acts 4:32.
16. Sister Laker notes that Aelred refers to St. Theodora of Alexandria described in the *Martyrology* (April 28, died in 491), following St. Ambrose, who, in *On Virgins* 2:4 erroneously reported the city of Antioch.
17. Cf. Psalms 39 [38]:6.
18. John 15:13.

(31–50): Charity and the Three Kinds of Friendship

Ivo inquires whether there is no distinction between charity and friendship. *Aelred* responds that the difference is vast. Far more are to be welcomed into the bosom of charity than are to be embraced by friendship, for the law of charity extends the embrace of love even to our enemies. It is only within the bonds of friendship, however, that we may share without fear the depths of our feelings and secrets of our hearts.

Ivo observes that there are many worldly people drawn to vice who seem to share similar bonds of friendship and find their bond sweeter than even the illicit pleasures and delights that they seek together. He asks Aelred to distinguish *spiritual* friendship from more base associations that share the name of friendship. *Aelred* responds that it is false to claim friendship among those who pursue a harmony of vices, since one who does not love is not a friend, and one who loves iniquity does not love his fellow-man, but "hates his own soul."[19] Indeed, he who does not love his own soul will be unable to love the soul of another.

Aelred proceeds to describe his version of three kinds of friendship, distinguishing true *spiritual* friendships from false *carnal* and *worldly* friendships. Mincing no words, he says that *carnal friendship* begins from the kind of affection which, like a prostitute, directs its step after any passerby.[20] A man aroused by the lust of the senses seeks a companion to further enkindle the flames of his heart as they form a sinful bond in pursuit of bodily pleasures. Such friendship is formed by ungoverned passions and not by the judgment of reason. It pursues illicit pleasures without moderation, and, as if inspired by furies, burns itself up and dissolves with the same thoughtlessness through which it was formed.

Worldly friendship, born of the desire for worldly advantages or gains, is always deceitful and full of intrigue, uncertain, inconstant, and insecure, for it changes with fortune and follows money. These are the fair-weather friendships described in the Scriptures: "For there is a friend who is such at his own convenience, but will not

---

19. Cf. Psalm 10:6 in the Vulgate or Douay-Rheims editions.
20. Cf. Ezekiel 16:25.

stand by you in your day of trouble."[21] When the hope of profit is gone, so is such a friend. The following lines sum it up well:

A friend not of the man, but of his purse is he,
Held fast by fortune fair, by evil made to flee.[22]

Still, Aelred notes that while worldly friendships are vicious, it is possible that they can lead some people to a certain measure of true friendship in that they may truly be harmonious in their hope of profits for one another. Yet such relationships are not true friendships if they start and continue merely on the basis of temporal benefits.

Spiritual friendship, the only one Aelred calls true, desires no worldly gains and seeks no extrinsic purpose, but arises from its own intrinsic dignity and the warmth of the human heart, so that its fruit and reward is nothing other than friendship itself. The Lord of the Gospel, after all, says, "I have appointed you that you should go and bear fruit,"[23] that is, to love one another. True friendship develops by perfecting itself, and the fruit brings the sweetness of the perfection. Aelred next provides a definition of spiritual friendship, building upon Cicero's definition:

And so spiritual friendship among the just is born of a similarity in life, morals, and pursuits, that is, it is a mutual conformity in matters human and divine united with benevolence and charity.[24]

Aelred is satisfied with this definition, but notes that "charity" is in accord with their Christian way of thinking in that it excludes all

---

21. Sirach 6:8.

22. Laker reported in her 1974 translation that the source of this quotation had not been traced at the time. The 2008 Braceland translation reads, "One who comes in good fortune and goes in misfortune / Loves not the person but the person's purse," and traces the lines to the Roman poet Ovid in his *Ex Ponto*, 2.3.23–24. Two centuries after Aelred, Geoffrey Chaucer included the sentiment of the verses from Sirach and Ovid in his *Monk's Tale*: "For he whose friends are friends of Fortune too, / Mishap will make them enemies I guess: / The proverb is both widely known and true."

23. John 15:16.

24. Laker's *Spiritual Friendship*, 61.

vice, and that "benevolence" denotes the loving feeling that is aroused and enjoyed interiorly. Such friendships not only include a harmony of opinions, but are perfected by the cardinal virtues, being directed by prudence, ruled by justice, guarded by fortitude, and moderated by temperance. Ivo, too, is satisfied, but he expresses one more concern. He would like to know the origin of friendship among men—whether it derived from nature or chance, was necessary in some way, or imposed upon the human race by some law.

(51–61): Friendship in the Beginning

Aelred responds that in his view, nature produces in humans the desire for friendship, experience enhances the desire, and human laws confirm it. God is all-powerful, all-good, self-sufficient and completely happy. Though he needs nothing outside of himself, he chose to give being, life, and intelligence to created things. It is God who gives all things their natures, and He has eternally willed and directed by his reason that peace be given to all of his creatures and that they be united in society, so that they, in their diversity, might show some trace of God's unity. Traces of this may be seen in inanimate things, in plants, and especially in animals, some of which are so eager to run about and play with one another that it would appear as if they operate through reason and prize friendship above all else! God's divine Wisdom also created many angels, so that they could experience the pleasant delights of companionship and love. While some are superior to others, envy would surely have ensued were it not prevented by the bonds of charity.

Finally, when God made man, he declared: "It is not good that the man should be alone. I will make him a helper fit for him."[25] To produce the highest inducement to charity and friendship, he fashioned the woman, not merely from similar material, but from the very substance of the man himself. The second human person came from the side of the first, so that nature itself would teach us of their equality, one neither superior nor inferior to the other, as is found in true friendship. Therefore, from the start, nature implanted within the heart of humankind a desire for friendship and charity,

---

25. Genesis 2:18.

which he tasted and found sweet. It was with the first man's Fall, however, that charity cooled and concupiscence worked stealthily to elevate man's private good over the common good. Friendship and charity became corrupted with the greed, envy, conflicts, rivalries, hates, and suspicions that accompany corrupted morals. Since no union of will and ideas is possible between the good and the wicked, friendship, which used to be shared by all like charity, became, by natural law, the province of only the few who were good.

These few, seeing the sanctity of law and society violated, bonded closer together in charity and rested in their joy. The wicked who despised virtue formed unions that they called friendship, but which did not deserve the name, and should have been distinguished from true friendship. True friendship is a natural thing that, like virtue and wisdom, should be sought out and preserved for its own sake, and those who possess them use them well and do not misuse them.

(62–68): The Wisdom of Friendship

At the mention of wisdom, *Ivo* asks whether many people do abuse wisdom, trying to please others through it, taking pride in themselves for having it, or considering it as a means of making money. *Aelred* replies with the words of "our" Augustine: "He who pleases himself, pleases a foolish man, because, to be sure, he is foolish who pleases himself."[26] The man who is foolish lacks wisdom, so how can he abuse that which he does not possess? Even proud chastity is not truly a virtue, because pride makes a vice of whatever is joined with itself.

Ivo rejoins that he still does not see why wisdom has been linked with friendship, since the two cannot be compared. *Aelred* replies that while they are not coequal, lesser things are often linked with greater things, and virtues admit of degrees. Widowhood, virginity, and conjugal chastity, for example, are greatly different as individual virtues, yet all share the commonality of being virtues. Though holy virginity is superior to both marriage and widowhood, its superiority does not make the other two less excellent. Indeed, Aelred believes that a close following of his arguments will reveal that

26. St. Augustine, *Sermon* 47:9ff. as cited in Laker.

friendship is almost nothing but wisdom. When one recalls that true friends love at all times, it is clear that friendship cannot endure without charity. "Since then in friendship eternity blossoms, truth shines forth, and charity grows sweet, consider whether you ought to separate the name of wisdom from these three."[27]

(69–71): God is Friendship?

Ivo then asks what he should make of all of this. Can we say of friendship what John, Jesus's friend, says of charity: "God is friendship?"[28]

Aelred replies that such a statement is unusual and is not itself found in Scripture, but he does not hesitate to accord to friendship what is accorded to charity in the second half of the verse, for "he that abides in friendship abides in God, and God in him."[29] This, Aelred promises, will be more clearly seen when they begin to discuss the fruits and benefits of friendship. Enough, he says, has been said for now, according to "the simplicity of our poor wit," and more must wait for another time.

Ivo then says his last words, not only of Book 1, but in all of Aelred's *Spiritual Friendship*, admitting that he is annoyed by having to wait, but that it is time for the evening meal, and that he knows that Aelred also has many responsibilities for the religious under his care.

Book II: The Fruits and Excellence of Friendship

(1–27): Friendship and the Spiritual Kiss of Christ

The discussion in Book II on the fruits and excellence that come from friendship is reported to take place some years later and after Ivo's death. A new friend, the somewhat irascible monk called *Walter*, waits to catch Aelred alone and asks him about his talk on spiritual friendship with Ivo many years ago. Walter has heard that, three days ago, the pages of notes from that discussion were found. *Aelred* allows Walter to read them in confidence, and he returns

27. Laker, 65.
28. Cf. 1 John 4:16.
29. Ibid.

after having read them, his ears now ready for Aelred's words. *Aelred* doubts his own ability to do the subject justice, but notes that Walter's hunger to learn is appropriate; nothing in human life is as holy, useful, difficult, sweet, and profitable as friendship, *for friendship bears fruit in this life and the next.*[30] Friendship's sweetness girds all virtues, conquers vices with its own virtue, alleviates adversity and tempers prosperity. Mankind can scarcely be happy at all without friendship, and a man who cannot enjoy it renders himself like a beast.

Aelred waxes eloquent on the joys and benefits of friendship in the words of Cicero and of Scripture and culminates, in section 14, by declaring that friendship borders on the perfection that consists in the love and knowledge of God. *When one becomes a friend of a man, he too becomes the friend of God,* in the very words of the Savior recorded in the Gospel: "No longer do I call you servants, but friends."[31]

In section 16, Aelred and Walter are joined by a young friend named Gratian. *Walter* declares that Gratian could be called friendship's child since all his energies seem focused on seeking to be loved and to love. He notes that Gratian might be eager to learn the difference between friendship and the counterfeit relationships that seem to be *spiritual* when they are truly merely *carnal.*

Aelred draws his friends' attention back to the idea that friendship is a stage or step toward the love and knowledge of God, and that there is nothing feigned, dishonest, or unholy about it, as is true of charity itself. Friendship, however, outshines charity in that those who share its bonds share all kinds of joys, delights, and charms, while the perfection of charity extends to those who prove burdensome and sorrowful to us. We feel true concern for such people, but do not admit them to the *intimacy* that characterizes friendship. Those in friendship are joined in honor, kindness, truth, joy, sweetness and good will, affection and action, all of which begin, grow, and are perfected in Christ.

Indeed, when a friend cleaves to a friend in the spirit of Christ,

30. Cf. 1 Timothy 4:8.
31. John 15:15.

they become one heart and one soul with him.[32] Ascending the steps of love to friendship with Christ, he is made one with him in one spiritual kiss, and his holy soul cries out: "Let him kiss me with the kiss of his mouth!"[33]

In a carnal kiss of the flesh there is a mingling of the breaths or spirits[34] as two spirits meet, blend, and unite, and a sweetness of mind and affection is born, binding the two together. There are *physical kisses* offered for appropriate reasons—for example, as a sign of reconciliation among enemies, a sign of peace in church, a sign of love between husband and wife as well as between friends long absent, or a sign of catholic unity when a guest is welcomed. *Spiritual kisses* are the kisses of friends made, not with touch of the mouth, but with the affection of the heart; they are not a joining of the lips, but a blending of the spirits by the purifying action of the Spirit of God. They emit a heavenly flavor. Aelred would call such kisses the kiss of Christ, which he offers, not through his own lips, but through the lips of another, breathing upon the friends that sacred affection so that it seems to them as if their two bodies shared in one spirit. They may then say with the Prophet, "See how good and pleasant it is for brethren to dwell together in unity."[35] The soul that has grown accustomed to this kiss knows that its sweetness comes from Christ and cries out, wishing that He would come in person delivering that kiss of grace: "Let him kiss me with the kiss of his mouth." With all its desires quieted thereby, the soul delights in that kiss of Christ alone, exclaiming, "His left hand is under my head and his right hand shall embrace me."[36]

(28–72): True Limits of True Friendship

Next, descending from such spiritual heights, Aelred responds to *Walter's* request for clarification on the limits of friendship in terms of how far one should go for a friend, since some think that there

---

32. Acts 4:32; cf. 1 Cor. 6:17.
33. Song of Solomon 1:2.
34. Latin, *spiritus*, for breath, or figuratively, spirit.
35. Ps. 133 [132]:1.
36. Song of Solomon 2:6.

should be no limits, even if the love of friendship should run counter to faith and honor, to common or private good.

Aelred replies that Christ provided the limit when he said, "Greater love has no man than this, that a man lay his life down for his friend."[37] Friends should be willing to die for one another. *Walter* wonders about wicked men who might take such joy in the harmony of their wicked intents that they would be willing to die for one another. Aelred expounds that friendship begins among the good, progresses among the best, and is consummated among the perfect. Anyone who delights in evil lacks the qualifications for friendship, because friendship springs forth and grows from one friend's esteem for the virtue of the other. He notes, too, that he does not intend to set up an impossible standard for "the good" to imply that they are completely perfect. Rather, by "the good" he means those who, within the limits of our mortal life, "live sober, upright, and godly lives in this world."[38] Aelred then condemns those who would shun the difficulties that might come with friendship, saying that Tully stated beautifully that "they seem to take the sun from the universe who take friendship out of life, for we have nothing better or more delightful from God."[39] He elaborates that we should strive to stay clear of relationships that merely resemble true friendship, such as the immature friendships of youth, which are passionate, fickle, fleeting, and unable to discern lawful from unlawful acts. Impure relationships such as these in adults are not spiritual friendship, but a poison to friendship, since they never contain the proper love that can link souls together and endure. They arise, rather, from concupiscence, corrupt true friendship, and lead men to neglect the things of the spirit for the things of the flesh. Therefore, the intentions of friendship must be pure from the start, guided by reason, and moderated by temperance. Friendships arising from such sweet attachment will produce true delights and hold fast over time. So-called friendships arising from evil intentions do not deserve the name.

37. John 15:13.
38. Titus 2:12.
39. Cf. *De Amicitia* 13:47.

As for the advantages of friendship, *Aelred* continues, such rewards should follow as consequences of friendship and not precede it as a preordained goal. Friendship is its own reward. He elaborates with examples of the friendships of King David, especially his relationship with Jonathan. David and Jonathan shared a sacred bond that did not arise because of desire for profit, but from esteem of one another's virtue—though both would enjoy its advantages, to the benefit of themselves and to posterity.[40]

Aelred concludes that divine authority has revealed to us that even the life of one's body should be laid down for a true friend. Since the life of the soul is far superior to the life of the body, no act should be performed for a friend that brings death to the soul—that is, through sin, which separates God from the soul and the soul from life.

Gratian thanks Walter for prompting such beneficial lessons from Aelred and requests that Aelred expound on what limits should be observed in maintaining friendships over time, but *Aelred* responds that an hour has flown by, and he must attend to other business. *Walter*, unhappy that their discussion is at an end, informs Aelred that he intends to return tomorrow to continue, concluding by warning Gratian that he'd better arrive on time!

Book III: How and Among Whom Friendships Can Endure

(1–20): Four Steps to Enduring Friendships

Responding to questions from Gratian and Walter, *Aelred* notes that the foundation of all spiritual love is the love of God. We must be careful that all of the affections we chose to pursue in friendship conform to that foundation, for while all of us are called to love everyone, not every person should be admitted into friendship. We must be careful whom we seek to become the companion of our soul. Adult friendships should be stable and enduring, not constantly changing like the friendships of children. Aelred then lists four steps which one must climb on the way to perfect friendship:

---

40. 1 Sam. 19–20; 2 Sam. 9.

(1) selection, (2) testing, (3) acceptance, and (4) *perfect harmony in matters human and divine, along with charity and benevolence.*[41]

As for selection, Aelred states that certain vices rule people out as potential friends unless they possess other pleasing virtues, in which case one should help them so that if they are healed they might become suitable as companions. He refers here to people who are irascible, fickle, suspicious, or excessively talkative. Scripture warns, "Make no friendship with a man given to anger, nor go with a wrathful man, lest you learn his ways."[42] Solomon adds: "Anger lodges in the breast of fools."[43] Who can maintain friendship with a fool?

At this point, *Walter* points out that Aelred himself was a devoted friend to an irascible man who offended him often, though Aelred did not once retaliate. *Aelred* replies that some people are irascible by natural temperament, but have accustomed themselves to restrain their emotions so that they do not fall into the five extreme vices that Scripture says destroy friendship.[44] When, at times, such a man lapses and offends a friend by a thoughtless word or act or through immoderate zeal, we must patiently bear with him. If he is a friend, we may gently or lightheartedly alert him to the offensiveness of his words or deeds.

(21–60) Five—No, Six—Vices that Destroy Friendship

Aelred derives his list of vices that destroy friendship from the Scriptures, noting that reconciliation among friends is possible except for cases of "slander, reproach, pride, disclosing of secrets, and a treacherous blow: for in all of these a friend will flee."[45]

---

41. Number 4 reiterates Cicero's definition of friendship in *De Amicitia*, 6:20.

42. Proverbs 22:24.

43. Eccles. 7:10.

44. Sirach 22:22. (Aelred will soon list and expound on each of these vices.)

45. Ibid. (Aelred uses the Latin Vulgate that provides separate words for the words translated above as "slander and reproach," while the Greek text has only one term, oneidismos, which is translated in the RSV as "reviling." I have bullet-pointed the five vices here for ease in examination.)

• *Slander*: It damages reputations and extinguishes love. Some men are so wicked that, even knowing that a statement uttered in a burst of anger may not be true, they will broadcast it as the truth. Such slander will appear credible, because it comes from one who knows his friend's secrets.

• *Reproach*: Many people delight to hear themselves praised and others discredited. Reproach from a friend is so impious that, even when false, it causes the innocent man to blush.

• *Pride*: What is harder to put up with than the arrogance of *pride*, when it disdains the humble submission of guilt that can heal damaged friendships? It renders one bold to hurl insults and indignant at admonishments.

• *Disclosing of Secrets*: There is nothing viler than the revelation of confidences held among friends. It leaves no love and tenderness between friends, but fills all with bitterness and poisons all with the venom of indignation, hatred, and suffering. Hence it is written: "Whoever betrays secrets destroys confidence, and he will never find a congenial friend."[46] Further, "whoever has betrayed secrets is without hope."[47]

• *Treacherous Blows*: The phrase "treacherous blow" refers to secret detraction, which is the hidden but mortal wound of an asp and a serpent. "If a serpent bite in silence," says Solomon, "he is no better who backbites secretly."[48]

Aelred notes that we should avoid people who display these vices

---

46. Sirach 27:16.

47. Sirach 27:21. Among the most poignant examples I have encountered of such a betrayal is found in the writings of St. Patrick of Ireland (c. AD 385–461). In his autobiographical *Confessio*, Patrick reports the anguish he felt, which hit him so hard that it was as if he were falling, when a man he considered his friend reported to church prelates in Britain a sin Patrick had revealed to him that had happened thirty years before, at the age of 15 and before his conversion to Christ. That the friend to whom he had revealed his soul in confessing the sin of his youth—the friend who had apparently shared his joy with him and told him, "Look, you are to be a bishop!"—would reveal his sin (its exact nature is unknown, though St. Patrick reports that it took less than an hour) in hopes of discrediting him was quite a jolt to him, though he thanked the Holy Spirit for keeping him from any similar sins since.

48. Eccles. 10:11.

unless they show that they are willing to repent. He provides examples of how erstwhile friends displayed such behaviors toward King David, and goes on to elaborate a few other personal characteristics that do not bode well for friendship—these including the *fickleness* of people who are too easily swayed in their opinions to remain constant in friendship, the *suspiciousness* that leads some people to always worry and imagine that their friend is plotting against them if he speaks in confidence to others, and the *excessive talkativeness* of the verbose, because a talkative man will not be justified.[49] Further, says the Wise One, "Do you see a man who is hasty in his words? There is more hope for a fool than him."[50]

The lesson here, per Aelred, is to seek out friends who are similar to us in their virtuous habits, recalling Ambrose's wise counsel: "Between the ill-matched, friendship cannot exist, and therefore, the graces of each such blend with the other."[51] Further, it is not necessary to find a man who *never* struggles with the character flaws noted above. Men who must fight such inclinations—stifling anger with patience, restraining levity with seriousness, and banishing suspicion by focusing on love—may become the most fitting of friends, having trained themselves to conquer vice with virtue.

Gratian then poses a personal question to Aelred, asking if he considers the aforementioned hotheaded friend of his to be irascible. *Aelred* responds that his friend is irascible indeed, but hardly so in friendship, pointing out that surely Gratian has never heard of strife between them. When Gratian presumes that this is due to Aelred's great patience, Aelred replies that he is mistaken; sometimes one's patience makes an angry man even angrier![52] Rather, he notes that when his irascible friend begins an angry outburst in public, he can restrain him by a mere nod of his head in his direction. His friend will stop himself, in midstream if need be, and wait until

---

49. Cf. Job 11:2.

50. Prov. 29:20.

51. Ambrose, *De Officiis*, 3. 133.

52. St. John Cassian in his *Conferences* 16:18 and Seneca in his *De Ira* 3:8 are among the theologians and philosophers who have noted how what we might today call "the silent treatment" in response to someone's anger can sometimes provoke yet more anger.

later to discuss the matter with Aelred in private. This man is worthy of praise, because he overcomes his natural inclinations on account of their friendship. Sometimes Aelred and his friend will disagree, but one will give in to the other, Aelred usually being the one to concede.

Further on in the narrative (at section 46), Aelred adds a sixth vicious circumstance that destroys friendship: *if a friend harms others one should love equally well and persists even when one confronts him.* In such a case, a friendship should be dissolved, for the love of friendship should not outweigh religion, faith, charity, love of one's neighbor, or the common welfare. Aelred notes, however, that while the bonds of intimacy within friendship may need to be dissolved, one's love for a former friend should endure.

(61–87): Four Qualities to be Tested in Friends

As *Gratian* declares that he will guard the door so that no one can interrupt them, *Aelred* moves from the *selection* of friends to revealing four qualities to be *tested* in friends along the way to formation of perfect friendships.

- *Loyalty*: One should be able to trust a friend with one's self and with all that belongs to one.
- *Right Intention*: A friend should seek nothing from friendship but God and friendship's natural goodness.
- *Discretion*: A friend should know what should be done on behalf of a friend, what it is proper to seek from a friend, what sufferings one should endure for a friend, when one's friend should be commended and when he should be corrected, and the right manner, time, and place for such correction.
- *Patience*: A friend should bear correction well and not come to hate the friend who corrects him, and be willing to bear all manner of hardships for his friend's sake.

Aelred declares that nothing surpasses the first quality of *loyalty*, for loyalty seems to be friendship's nurse and guardian. Although loyalty may be hidden in times of prosperity, it becomes conspicuous in adversity. Aelred cites several Scriptural verses from Solomon in support of this truth, including the following: "A friend loves at all times and a brother is tested in adversity," and "trust in a faithless man in time of trouble is like a bad tooth or a foot that slips."[53]

As for the second quality of *right intention*, Aelred sums up the guidance our Lord and Savior himself on the proper love of friendship: "You shall love your neighbor as yourself."[54] Aelred adds that this is "the mirror": we must love ourselves, especially if we love God and are worthy of spiritual friendship. Of course, we expect no reward from ourselves for our self-love, for self-love is natural and dear to each one of us. Unless we can transfer this generous, gratuitous love from ourselves to others, we cannot savor the true friendship that comes when the friend that we love is like another self.

Elaborating on the third and fourth qualities of *discretion* and *patience,* there are some men so perverse and shameless that they expect a friend to possess a character superior to their own.[55] These men are impatient with the trivial faults of their friends, lack the good judgment to determine what is important, and become indignant over petty things. If we fail to test for discretion and acquire an impudent friend, we set ourselves up for hassles and disputes. A friend without prudent discretion is like a ship without a pilot, changing course with every shift in the winds. There are many opportunities to test a friend's ability to endure correction, and at times such correction should be harsh on purpose, so that his patience will be tried and revealed.[56]

(88–126): On the Cultivation of Friendship

Having admitted into our friendship a person who has passed these tests of character, *Aelred* provides a quick survey of a variety of virtues and behaviors that serve to cultivate friendship and ensure its stability. These include *frankness, congeniality,* and *sympathy,* all of which relate to loyalty. People who are crafty and duplicitous cannot be loyal, and those who are unmoved by another's concerns will not be reliable. A friend must display a *pleasant tone of voice,* a

---

53. Proverbs 17:17; 25:19.
54. Matt. 22:39.
55. Cicero, *De Amicitia*, 22:82.
56. Ibid., 24:88.

cheerful look, gentle manners, and a *serene look in the eyes,* for such qualities add great relish to friendship. There are times for being solemn, but friendships should be free and relaxed, inclined toward congeniality and approachableness without undue levity or dissipation.[57]

Aelred expounds at length, and with many citations from the first book of Samuel, on the ideal and enduring friendship shared between King David and Jonathan. He echoes Cicero in addressing many other issues related to friendship, such as the relationship between friends of superior and inferior status (like that of David and Jonathan), as well as the question of what friends should do to benefit one another, eagerly anticipating each other's needs.

In answer to *Walter's* question about whether the monk's prohibition from giving or bestowing gifts does not take the charm out of friendship, *Aelred* declares that it was a wise man who said that men would live happy lives if the words "mine" and "yours" were removed from their midst.[58] Indeed, holy poverty itself bestows great strength upon spiritual friendship, that poverty being holy precisely because it is voluntary. Avarice kills friendships, and friendships endure best when the friends' souls are cured of this pest. Monks can still bestow great gifts to their spiritual friends by showing concern for one another, praying for each other, feeling shame at each other's failure and rejoicing at each other's successes, grieving over another's fall as if it were their own, and considering another's progress as theirs. By any means possible, a friend should lift the weak, support the infirm, console the suffering, and calm the wrathful. He should also respect his friend so much that he dare not do anything disgraceful in his friend's presence, lest his friend's soul be troubled. Aelred reports that many a time a mere nod from a friend has extinguished the flames of his own anger. We must treat our friends with reverence, kindly correcting or even reproving them if necessary, and stand willing for our own correction or reproval.

Later, *Walter* asks Aelred about giving honors, promotions, and privileges to friends, and on what basis they should be awarded.

---

57. Ibid., 18:66.
58. Pseudo-Seneca, *Monita,* 97.

Aelred echoes Cicero in saying we should be concerned not so much with what we can bestow as with what our friend can handle, and provides the illuminating example of how Christ, in promoting Peter as the most fitting leader of the apostles, did not by any means diminish his affection for John, his beloved disciple. To Peter he entrusted his Church; to John his beloved Mother.[59] To Peter he gave the keys to the kingdom;[60] to John he revealed the secrets of his heart. Peter was thereby more exalted, but John more secure from anxiety.

(127–134): The Ladder of Friendship Ascends to and Descends from Christ

Aelred goes on to relate the benefits and joys that he has obtained from spiritual friendship, saying that they are a foretaste of the eternal friendships which we will share in heaven. We ascend the ladder of charity to embrace Christ himself and descend to rest in the love of our neighbor. Friendship, then, should be cultivated as a means to spiritual perfection, as friends grow in virtue together and pray for one another in Christ. When we focus on our love of Christ in our prayers for our friends, the affections begin to meld into one another, and through our close contact with Christ, the friend begins to taste Christ's sweetness and experience how dear He is.

Aelred concludes as he started, with Christ. When the holy love with which a man embraces a friend ascends to embrace Christ, he will experience the joyful fruits of friendship while he waits for their fullness in the life to come. When we finally come to embrace the supreme and eternal good, spiritual friendship, to which we can now admit only a few, will be poured out to all and will flow back to God from all, and God will be all in all.[61]

59. John 19:26.
60. Matt. 16:19.
61. 1 Cor. 15:28.

6

Aelred's Christocentric
Legacy of *Spirituali Amicitia*

It is Aelred, not Cicero, who makes friendship seem something so time-less and universal that one is tempted to ignore its historical context.
⁓Brian Patrick McGuire, *Friendship and Community*[1]

AELRED OF RIEVAULX produced a truly remarkable contribution to and transformation of the classical philosophical conceptions of friendship. We will begin by briefly examining its precursors and motivations, both in the literature of friendship that preceded him and in the details of Aelred's own life.

All Things New in Christ: What to
Make of Friendship in Light of Christianity?

We saw in our legacy chapter on Cicero that early Church Fathers, including Sts. Ambrose, Jerome, and Augustine, knew and were impacted by Cicero's writings, including those on friendship. While Augustine wrote of the pros and cons of intimate friendships in his autobiographical *Confessions*, Jerome's friendships, some quite tumultuous, are documented in his many surviving letters, and Ambrose included a small section on friendship inspired by Cicero at the end of his book *On the Duties of the Clergy*. Still, as Christ had revolutionized the world shortly after the death of Cicero, Christianity gave rise to significant differences of opinion regarding the value

---

1. Brian Patrick McGuire, *Friendship and Community: The Monastic Experience,* 350–1250 (Ithaca, NY: Cornell University Press, 2010), 326.

of human friendships, even the virtuous and harmonious kinds described by the pre-Christian pagan thinkers Aristotle and Cicero.

In the first several centuries after Christ, many Greek Fathers of the Church in the East and their followers left urban life and sought perfection in solitude in the deserts, either as solitary anchorites (hermits) or as cenobites (monks) who shared some form of communal life apart from the rest of society. In the West, there were some holy hermits, but Latin Fathers such as St. Benedict helped establish a strong and enduring monastic tradition of separation from the world within the communal setting of the monastery. Some saw Christ's call for universal love of even our enemies as contrary to the special, individual attention that bespeaks personal friendships. Christ proclaimed in his sermon on the mount, "for if you love those who love you, what reward do you have?" (Matt. 5:46). Further, St. James wrote, "Do you not know that friendship with the world is enmity with God? Therefore, whoever wishes to be a friend of the world makes himself an enemy of God" (Jas. 4:4). Many theologians in the East and the West interpreted these words as a condemnation, not only of inappropriate *worldliness*, but of individual *friendships* in the world. They believed that when a man left the world to embrace the life of spiritual perfection, friendships and family ties should be severed and not replaced within their new life of the spirit.

So-called "particular friendships" within a monastery were also commonly perceived as a threat to the unity of communal monastic life. Such personal bonds might encourage monks to form exclusive cliques or abbots to play favorites among the men under their charge. Still, friendship was certainly not frowned upon everywhere, and particular personal friendships clearly formed and thrived at times. Even St. Benedict's Rule, though it does not explicitly address friendships, directs that the abbot is not to love one monk more than another "*unless* he finds one who is better in good actions and obedience."[2] This would seem to open the door to friendships of virtue, at least between a superior and an inferior.

---

2. Rule of St. Benedict, chapter 2:16–17 as cited in McQuire, 82. (The italics are in McQuire's text.)

In his masterful survey of monasticism and friendship, medieval historian Brian Patrick McGuire has chronicled the evidence for the existence of *writings about friendship* and *friendships* themselves from the 4th century AD until and beyond the time of Aelred in the 12th century. The evidence comes largely from correspondences in which the parties address one another as friends and discuss their own relationships or friendship in general. Another common source is that of hagiographies, the stories of saint's lives, in which friendships may or may not be addressed.

Along with a host of lesser-known names from across the centuries, the friendly letter-writers include Charlemagne's educated adviser Blessed Alcuin (c. 735–804), St. Anselm of Bec and Canterbury (1033–1109), known in philosophical circles for his fascinating "ontological proof" of the existence of God but also the author of a prayer for friends, and St. Bernard of Clairvaux (1090–1153), who descended upon the monastic life with a group of his own friends, reformed the Cistercian Order, and ordered St. Aelred to complete *The Mirror of Charity,* his masterwork on love and the monastic life and the precursor to *Spiritual Friendship.* In fact, the letter from Bernard to Aelred commanding him "in the name of Jesus Christ and in the Spirit of our God" to write *The Mirror of Charity* is reproduced at the beginning of that work.

As for the hagiographies, McGuire posits that prevailing ideas about friendship in particular periods in time can be discerned from contemporary accounts of the lives of the saints. For example, while spiritual men of the tenth century were typically admired for their solitude, a century later their friendships are described in favorable terms. Yet one century more and the *Vita Gundulf* (written from 1114 to 1124, in Aelred's lifetime) dwells in detail on the friendship between the bishops Gundulf (1077–1108) and the aforementioned Anselm of Canterbury.

By the time of Aelred's youth, friendship was in the air within monasteries as well as in the outside world. Writings mentioning friendship were popular among learned monks and clerics. These commonly included phrases from classical literature, most notably from Cicero, and often featured the terse definition of Roman historian Sallust (86–35 BC), who wrote that friendship is "to like and

dislike the same things," repeating the important element of concordance or harmony of wills emphasized by Aristotle before him
and Cicero after. Within this monastic literature, too, an important
new element is visible in the incorporation of scriptural stories and
doctrines within the Old and New Testaments, which served to provide examples of holy friendships and encouragement towards
forming them. Still, we know of no entire work specifically focusing
on friendship within the Christian world until the time of Aelred's
Spiritual Friendship in the mid-12th century.

Aelred would prove to be a master synthesizer of classical and
scriptural, political and monastic, virtuous and "spiritual" friendships. In this he did not merely combine, but enhanced and transformed the idea of friendship from something that might be
tolerated within the bounds of Christian charity and monastic community to something with the power to draw us toward perfect love
of Christ, providing in its sweetness a foretaste of heavenly bliss.

Aelred of Rievaulx: From the
Kitchen of the King to the Cloister of God

After Aelred's death on January 12, 1167, a *Vita Aelredi* (Life of Aelred) was written by Walter Daniel, very likely the same irascible
Walter we met in books II and III of the *Spiritual Friendship*. After a
greeting to an abbot, Walter begins with a dramatic flair that speaks
of the two men's own spiritual friendship:

> Our father is dead; he has vanished from our world like the morn-
> ing sunshine, and many hearts long that this great light should
> flood with its brightness the memory of generations to come, and
> indeed for those still living for whom it shone in all its splendor.[3]

The book is an intriguing and informative read, but some modern
historians have noted that our most reliable guide to Aelred's life is
found in Aelred's own writings. Here I will provide a few details of

---

3. Walter Daniel, *The Life of Aelred of Rievaulx*, F.M. Powicke, trans. (Kalamazoo, MI: Cistercian Press, 1994), 89.

the life of Aelred, since, though far less widely known than Aristotle, Cicero, and St. Thomas Aquinas, he was the most self-revealing of the four, and friendships clearly played a central role in his own life.

Aelred's father Eliaf was a married priest descended from a line of married priests in a day when clerical celibacy was becoming the norm, under the reforms of Pope Gregory VII and, in England, the encouragement of William the Conqueror. When Eliaf had to leave the shrine of St. Cuthbert in Durham in which he and his ancestors had served, he moved to Hexham in the north of England in 1083, where Aelred was born in 1110. In 1138, Eliaf became a monk at the cathedral monastery of St. Cuthbert in the presence of his three sons, one of whom, Aelred, had become a monk four years before. We know, too, that Aelred had a sister, and McGuire has provided interesting glimpses of Aelred's brotherly advice to her in still-extant letters.

Though he was the son of a priest, Aelred's youth had a quite worldly bent. Probably because of his family's important connections through the Church, he was sent to the court of King David I of Scotland (1084–1153) at around the age of fifteen. There he befriended the king's three sons, including Henry, the heir apparent. Aelred was well liked and successful at court as a young man, though he would later belittle his importance, declaring that he was but the steward of the king's kitchen. Walter Daniel has supplied his title there as "*dappifer summus*" (chief steward), but his exact duties are not known. Still, he was clearly favored by the king, and in his early twenties, in 1132, he was sent out on some business involving Archbishop Thurstan of York, during which time he visited the Cistercian abbey at Rievaulx. He was so taken by his day with the monks that, after sleeping on the decision a single night, he presented himself at Rievaulx for admittance as a monk. In the ensuing years, the young monk was sent to Rome to help with negotiations regarding Archbishop Thurstan's successor and had a fateful meeting with St. Bernard of Clairvaux on his way back. By age thirty-three, he was sent to lead a group of monks in founding a new abbey at Revesby, and at age thirty-seven in 1147, he was called back to Rievaulx as their abbot, a position he held until his death twenty years later. Abbot Aelred ruled the monastery, wrote a number of spiritual and historical books, and clearly developed and cherished his own spiritual friendships all the while.

Modern authors have argued that Aelred's writings on friendship and other details of his life prove that he was a repressed and conflicted soul of homosexual orientation. Aelred, for example, did not discourage monks from showing simple physical signs of affection at times, such as the clasping of hands. He speaks, at times, in rich, sensual physical imagery, such as when he compares the physical, the spiritual and the intellectual kiss. When Aelred specifically mentions homosexual acts in his writings, however, he condemns them as sinful. Further, his use of sensual imagery, most particularly in reference to the Song of Songs (otherwise known as the Song of Solomon or the Canticle of Canticles), has a long history within the writings of the Church for its spiritual symbolism. I will not enter the fray except to note that several sober scholars I have encountered are of the opinion that there is insufficient evidence one way or the other, and that, regardless of what his own orientation may or may not have been, Aelred clearly writes of intimate *spiritual* unions in his writings on friendship and love and never of genital sexual acts.

Aelred suffered from many physical ailments in his middle age and later years—indeed, today he is considered a patron saint of sufferers from bladder stones. In the last years of his life, he was allowed to live in a little cell of his own within the infirmary, where groups of up to twenty or thirty monks would cram themselves to converse with him. Aelred died surrounded by such a circle of spiritual friends on Thursday, January 12, 1167.

Book 1 Commentary: The Nature of Spiritual Friendship

Since Aelred's own writing is usually clear and always beautiful, and because of its overlap with Cicero's *De Amicitia*, my commentaries on the books of Aelred's dialogues will be brief, mainly intended to highlight new insights and to send readers to Aelred's own work. With that said, the most important and unique feature of Aelred's *Spiritual Friendship* jumps to the fore in the very first sentence when he declares his hope that a third person, namely Christ, is present with himself and Ivo. Although he does not cite the verse,

Aelred demonstrates a familiarity with the declaration of Christ that "where two or three are gathered together, there am I in the midst of them" (Matt. 18:20). This presence of Christ is something that Aristotle and Cicero never wrote about or thought about, having died before Christ's birth. Though Aelred notes openly that he owes much to Cicero for his understanding of friendship, his friendship with Jesus Christ has totally transformed the meaning of friendship for him, making it immeasurably more "*dulcis*"—more sweet, dear, and delightful to him. Aelred is about to present his case that Christ did not come to abolish friendship, but to fulfill it! It is God become man, Jesus Christ, who forges the bonds between human beings in friendships that center on Him and His love.

Though Aelred starts with the loftiest of thoughts, he clearly shows that we will not be lost in abstractions as he perceptively comments on his friend Ivo's body language and gestures. Here is the stuff of human friendship lived. Aelred notes and interprets the look in Ivo's eyes, his facial expressions, his bodily movements; Ivo responds that his interpretations were correct, and no doubt were prompted by the spirit of grace and charity moving within Aelred. We will not be mired in logical analyses or oratorical self-displays in this treatment of friendship; instead, we will experience friendship in action. Aelred quickly declares that the discussion between himself and Ivo will be just that—a discussion among friends, and not a lecture from a superior.

Aelred also makes clear how Christocentric their discussion will be, declaring that friendship must begin with Christ, continue with Christ, and be perfected by Christ. Ivo wisely proposes that they begin by defining their terms, and requests a definition of friendship. Aelred responds, in section 11 of the text, with Cicero's definition of friendship as "*mutual harmony in affairs human and divine coupled with benevolence and charity.*"

Aelred then considers the significance of key words, including charity and benevolence, and how they encompass both the affections and actions found in friendship. He notes in section 21 that friendship is the virtue by which spirits are bound together in love and sweetness, and out of many become one. In section 26, Aelred addresses Ivo's despair of attaining true friendship because of all the difficulties involved, citing the maxim that striving for great things is itself a great thing. He notes further that virtuous minds will continually ponder lofty and fine thoughts, whether to help them attain what they desire or to better understand what they ought to desire.[4]

In this section, Aelred also introduces a Christian understanding of virtue that is not to be found in Aristotle or Cicero. Aristotle wrote that to build enduring dispositions toward virtue we must repeatedly perform acts of virtue, as men become builders by building and harpists by playing the harp. Aelred, however, notes that Christians need not despair of acquiring the virtues necessary for true friendship, because virtue is there for the asking: "Ask and you shall receive…" (Matt. 7:7, Jn. 16:24). It is Christ himself, the source and bond of Christian friendship, who spoke these words to us. We see the same advice applied to that highest virtue of wisdom in James: "If anyone of you lacks wisdom, let him ask God, who gives to all men generously and without reproaching, and it will be given him" (Jas. 1:5). Aelred would not deny, however, that we must play our part in cooperating with such gracious gifts. His treatise on friendship is focused on the actions that friends must perform to build and sustain spiritual friendships.

In section 28, Aelred makes the bold declaration that, while Cicero in his time wrote that only three or four notable friendships had been proclaimed throughout history, Christians are able to cite *thousands* of friendships made possible through Christ's grace. Interestingly, the first such relationship that he cites is a friendship between a man and a woman—the martyr Theodora and the soldier Didymus, who died trying to save her. Aelred here references John 15:13, when Christ proclaimed that there is no greater love than to lay down one's life for one's friend.

In section 31, Ivo asks whether vicious people may also delight in friendship. Aelred's response is buttressed by Scripture and echoes

---

4. Though Aelred does not cite them, the statement calls to mind these words of St. Paul: "Finally brethren, whatever is true, whatever is honorable, whatever is just, whatever is pure, whatever is gracious, if there is an excellence, if there is anything worthy of praise, think about these things" (Phil. 4:8).

ideas in his own *Mirror of Charity* as well as Aristotle's conclusions on self-love: true friendship is not possible among the wicked, because they do not truly love themselves and are therefore unfit for loving others.

In section 32 Aelred distinguishes charity from friendship, since the love of charity should be extended to all, while friendship's embrace is limited. Charity and the other virtues are necessary conditions for the production of true, spiritual friendship. Aelred then provides us with a variation on the three kinds of friendship we saw spelled out by Aristotle, delineating not friendships of pleasure, use, and virtue, but *carnal, worldly,* and *spiritual* friendships. He describes *carnal* (of the flesh) friendships as focused upon the mutual enjoyment of vice, *worldly* friendships as focused upon hopes of gain, and *spiritual* friendships as focused upon similar lifestyles, character, and goals among good people. In spiritual friendships, the word *charity* is meant in the Christian sense, meaning that it drives out and excludes vice. This is why spiritual friends may safely share their secrets with one another. Aelred also makes note, in 48, of the role played by *harmony of desire* in spiritual friendships, referring to Sallust's maxim that friends like and dislike the same things. The more sincere such friendships are, the pleasanter; the holier they are, the sweeter.

Another uniquely Christian lens is applied to friendship after Ivo asks about its origins in section 50. Aelred responds, as did Aristotle and Cicero before him, that the desire for friendship is impressed by nature within the human soul. Yet he proceeds to provide a Christian perspective, arguing that, while God is totally sufficient in himself, he made his creatures—men and angels above all others—to derive joy from the love of friendship. Here he inserts an observation that other theologians have made about Eve's creation from Adam's rib, with a special application to friendship: that Eve was made from Adam's side illustrates the equality between men and women, so that relationships between them are not the friendships between unequals, or superiors and inferiors, that Aristotle and Cicero wrote about. It was only after the sin of the Fall that the evil desires of concupiscence entered into the picture, so that people would seek their own private good from others rather than the common good born of friendship. The virtues of wisdom and charity provide the means to overcome this tendency toward sin and to embrace others in loving relationships.

At the end of book one, Ivo proposes the striking question of whether we can say of friendship what Jesus's friend John said of charity: "God is friendship."[5] Aelred hedges a bit, noting that the idea is not explicitly Scriptural, yet he agrees—paraphrasing the second half of the verse—that one who abides in friendship does indeed abide in God. It is a thought that clearly elevates spiritual friendship to a supreme spiritual good. Some modern commentators have noted that this could have provided an opportunity for Aelred to discuss friendship as it applies to the three persons of the Holy Trinity, but he does not go in this direction. His treatise is Christ-centered nonetheless, with a clear focus on how Christ invites and enables us to grow in friendship, through, with, and in him.

Book 2 Commentary: Fruits that Spring from Spiritual Friendship

In section 8, Walter comments on the delicious sweetness of the fruits of friendship. Aelred responds by providing a rich paean to friendship as the foundation of all virtues, destroyer of all vice, and key to happiness. This is a thought worthy of reflection today. Do our own friendships serve to build us and our friends up in virtue? Do we aid one another in overcoming weakness and vice?

In section 14, Aelred notes that while friendship is like glory to the rich, tax relief to the poor, and medicine to the sick, its greatest benefit exceeds all of these and rises close to the perfection that consists in the knowledge and enjoyment of God. Through spiritual friendship we become friends with God. Again, Aelred cites the words of our friend Christ Himself: "No longer do I call you servants . . . but friends" (John 15:15).

Walter is so stirred by Aelred's observations that he declares that he is hardly even alive if he lacks such lofty fruits of friendship, and that Aelred's description of friendship as a stage close to spiritual perfection has nearly made him forget all his cares for things of the earth.

---

5. Paraphrasing 1 John 4:16: "God is love."

By section 16, Gratian has joined in, and the men's discussion moves on towards the intimacy, truth, joy, and charm that friendship supplies when it begins, proceeds, and is perfected in Christ. Here, Aelred moves into the metaphorical language of the spiritual kiss, citing Song of Solomon 1:2: "Let him kiss me with the kiss of his mouth." Aelred clarifies that he means no physical kiss, but a spiritual kiss—a meeting not of the lips, but of hearts, the word *spiritus* meaning "breath" as well as spirit or soul. Purified by the Spirit of God, such a kiss emits a heavenly flavor and can be called the kiss of Christ. Such a kiss between friends is a sharing and unification of souls and a source of joy, as we see declared by the Prophet David: "Behold, how good and pleasant it is when brothers dwell in unity!" (Ps. 133 [132]:1).

Descending from such lofty heights, Aelred returns to consider carnal and worldly friendships, and declares in section 66 that they are really hardly worthy of consideration. The limits of true friendships, in which each friend values the other for his own sake, were laid down by Christ: one should be willing to lay down his life for his friend, valuing that friend more than his own body. Aelred makes clear, however, that as the soul is more important than the body, a friend should never do something gravely evil for a friend, for to do so would be to bring about the death of his soul and separation from God. The hour has passed, and it is time to take another look at the third and last dialogue.

Book 3 Commentary: The Chaff That May Grow Among the Wheat in Spiritual Friendship

Here, a good dozen or so pages into this chapter, we encounter *Spiritual Friendship*'s last and longest book. Aelred starts by proclaiming that the source and origin of friendship is love, and that, while there can be love without friendship, there is no friendship without love. How, then, are we to form friendship based on love, and what do we do when a spiritual friendship has, so to speak, lost that loving feeling?

In the spirit of brevity we will zoom in on the fact that, in tying up loose ends on the formation and preservation of true friendships and the pitfalls along the way, this is where Aelred gets numerical, so to speak. Let us briefly recall several sets of numbered lists he expounds to Walter and Gratian before he reaches his summit on the *summum bonum* of the spiritual life that is spiritual friendship.

Four Steps to Enduring Friendships

1. Selection
2. Testing or Probation
3. Acceptance or Admission
4. Perfect Harmony with Charity and Benevolence

For Aelred, spiritual friendship is not to be undertaken lightly. It provides potential for great blessings, but also for great harm if the friendships are formed with people who do not truly seek out virtue. We are surely shaped, for better or for worse, by the company we keep. Further, friends share their hearts with one another, so that few things hurt more than betrayal by a friend. Aelred's four steps are the stairs we must climb to reach the perfect pinnacle of spiritual friendship. Special care must be taken when choosing and observing the behaviors of potential friends in those first two stages, because perfect friendship can only exist among good people. Once a friend is accepted, you are his and he is yours, in body and soul, for the duration.

Six Vices That Destroy Friendship

1. Slander
2. Reproach
3. Pride
4. Disclosing of Secrets
5. Acts of Treachery
6. Acts of Harm against Others We Love

Both Aristotle and Cicero addressed the possibility that, in friendships of virtue, one party may reject virtue, so that the friendship must be dissolved. Unique to Aelred is his analysis of vices particularly deadly to friendship, based on Scripture: "If thou has opened a sad mouth, fear not, for there may be a reconciliation: except upbraiding, and reproach, and pride, and disclosing of secrets, or a treacherous wound: for in all these cases a friend will flee away" (Sirach 22:22).[6] In this verse we find the first five vices which are deadly to friendship. The sixth occurs when a friend deliberately harms, and will not desist in harming, another or others we love. Aelred's reason for including this vice is spelled out in section 46—the particular love of friendship, important as it is, cannot outweigh religion, loyalty, love of fellow citizens, or the common good.

Four Qualities to be Tested in Friends

1. Loyalty or Faithfulness
2. Right Intention
3. Discretion or Judgment
4. Patience

Aelred's list of four qualities to be tested in friends might raise some modern eyebrows. Should friends put friends to the test? In Luke 4:12, echoing Deuteronomy 6:16, Jesus tells us not to put *God* to the test. Nonetheless, starting in section 61, Aelred echoes Cicero in his recommendation of testing friends, citing Proverbs that do indeed advise us to test friends (Proverbs 27:17; 25:19). He spells out four ways of testing friends and the reason for each. *Loyalty* or *faithfulness* should be tested, so that we may know if we can trust the friend with our important secrets. To test a friend's *right intention*, we must strive to find out if he is seeking nothing other than God and good from our friendship. Here, Aelred recalls Christ's second great commandment: to love one's neighbor as oneself. *Discretion* or *judgment* is tested when we determine what our friend believes should be done for a friend, the burdens to be born, the kinds of deeds that warrant congratulations, and his willingness to be corrected if need be. *Patience* is tested when we observe his actual response to a rebuke

---

6. I have provided this as rendered in the Douay-Rheims edition, a translation most similar to the Latin Vulgate Aelred would have used. The book of Sirach is named Ecclesiasticus there. If the first words seem unclear, the RSV begins "If you have opened your mouth against your friend. . . ."

of friendly correction or to a burden placed on him by our friendship.

On the Friendliness That Grows Fruitful Friendships

Aelred extensively addresses the various pitfalls found in friendships due to a lack of or lapses in virtue. Yet, again echoing Cicero, he also details in depth, beginning in section 88, the behaviors and character traits that tend to make friendships thrive—traits essential to what we could call *affability* or simply *friendliness*. These include:

- Loyalty
- Frankness
- Congeniality
- Sympathy
- Pleasant tone of voice
- Cheerful demeanor
- Gentle or courteous manners
- A serene or tranquil look in the eyes
- A sense of levity or humor

We might ask ourselves to what extent we display such traits to our own friends. Do we, perhaps, manifest some of these traits with some friends and some of them with others? Which ones might we improve on in ourselves, in order to improve our relationships with our "second selves"?

Spiritual Friendship Through, With, and In Christ

Aelred concludes as he begins and emphasizes throughout, explaining that spiritual friendship is ultimately friendship with, through, and in Christ. We climb the ladder of friendship and see Christ; strengthened by His love, we descend that ladder and share that love with our spiritual friends. Aristotle argued that we would not want a virtuous friend to become a god, yet Aelred experienced his deepest friendship with a completely sinless and virtuous man, who is God incarnate.

The Death and Rebirth of Spiritual Friendship after the Death and Rebirth of St. Aelred

Despite the beauty and profundity of Aelred's *Spiritual Friendship,* it did not become widely known and disseminated among Christendom in the centuries following his death. Most copies remained in England. McQuire reports that only a single copy was found in the large library of the Cistercian Abbey of Clairvaux in France, and that one not obtained until the 13th Century. This is especially striking when one recalls that St. Bernard of Clairvaux had himself commissioned Aelred's earlier masterwork, *The Mirror of Charity,* and that a letter from him graced its first pages. Bernard had passed away in 1153, though, before Aelred wrote *Spiritual Friendship.*

Douglass Roby reports that by the end of the fourteenth century, at least, four abridged versions of *Spiritual Friendship* existed, one of which was mistakenly attributed to St. Augustine.[7] Another text, extant in the 13th century and particularly popular in Spain, combined the texts of *The Mirror of Charity* and *Spiritual Friendship.* Perhaps most intriguing of all is a 13th-century text of Peter of Blois that essentially rewrites both texts, adding the kind of flowery language that had then become popular, but does not acknowledge Aelred as the author. Roby declares it "full scale plagiarism,"[8] noting that its authorship was even erroneously attributed to Roman statesman and author Cassiodorus (AD 485–585) in some manuscripts of the day!

Perhaps due to changes in attitudes toward friendships within the monastery and the rise of the mendicant religious orders, universities, and scholasticism in the ensuing centuries, *Spiritual Friendship* was not widely known, and other monks were not inspired to write such treatises of their own. It was not until the 1940s that English translations first appeared. Both modern historian McGuire and modern translator Mark F. Williams note, quoting different sources, that the *Spiritual Friendship* was suppressed until relatively recent times within the famous Cistercian of the Strict Observance (aka

---

7. In the Introduction to previously cited Laker translation of *Spiritual Friendship,* 38.

8. Ibid., 39.

Trappist) Monastery in Gethsemani, Kentucky.[9] Thankfully, in the 1960s an explosion of interest in the writings of St. Aelred, including the *Spiritual Friendship*, occurred, at least within the Cistercian Order.

Which of Aelred's insights might the modern Christian reader take and run with in order to better run toward Christ, sped along on his or her course by special spiritual "second selves"? What joy might be gleaned from Aelred's idea that in heaven there will be more than enough time, and such an abundance of purified souls, that spiritual friendship will be shared, not just between a few, but between all whom Christ has called not his servants, but his friends?

Leaving such questions for readers to ponder, we will move now to the last of our four friendships and four friends—the saintly man, and "Angelic Doctor," who brought Christ to Aristotle's friendship, as Aelred did to Cicero's.

9. McGuire (page 331) notes that he was told in person, by the Cistercian Chrysogonus Waddell at a conference in 1984, that the order forbad reading the work to novice and young monks until the 1950s. Williams (page 21) cites a written statement from Thomas Merton, noting that until recently Aelred's book was kept there under lock and key. (I write with no disrespect whatsoever intended for the monastery at Gethsemani. Indeed, I write today on Christmas Eve, 2016, in anticipation of partaking tomorrow of a gift to my family from that very same place, their holy and wholly delicious Kentucky bourbon chocolate walnut fudge!)

PART IV

St. Thomas Aquinas's Charitable Friendship

✝

If we speak of the happiness of this life, the happy man needs friends.
St. Thomas Aquinas, *Summa Theologica*

7

Charitable Friendship
in the *Summa Theologiae*

It is written (John 15:15) I will not now call you servants ... but My friends. Now this was said to them by reason of nothing else than charity. Therefore charity is friendship.

St. Thomas Aquinas, *Summa Theologica*, II-II, Q. 23, a.1

CHRISTIAN THEOLOGIAN Tertullian (c. 155–240) famously (or infamously) asked, "What has Athens to do with Jerusalem?," and further, "What has the Academy to do with the Church?" Clearly, Sts. Aelred and Thomas Aquinas knew that well-reasoned philosophy contained many gems well worth the mining and polishing by those in the Church. Indeed, as St. Aelred of Rievaulx's writings constituted a Catholic cathedral of friendship built of stones quarried from Cicero's Roman forum, so too did St. Thomas Aquinas's writings produce yet another Catholic cathedral, built upon the edifice of Aristotle's Athenian Lyceum.

Before we dig into summaries of St. Thomas's writings on friendship in this chapter, I will note that, while he did not write any complete work specifically focused on friendship, he considered the topic many times, from many angles, within his *Summa Theologica* and many other works. In this chapter I have summarized his writings touching on friendship, addressed in Questions 23–27 of his writings on the charity in part II of the *Summa Theologica*. These five questions are comprised of a total of 53 thoroughly developed articles on specific questions within the general heading of each question. For Question 23—"Charity, Considered in Itself, Article I,

Whether Charity is Friendship"—I have summarized the give-and-take arrangement St. Thomas uses for all of the articles within each question, starting with objections, moving to an *"On the Contrary"* section, and followed by an *"I answer that"* in which St. Thomas provides his own answer, replying to the objections one by one. For brevity and clarity, I have simply culled highlights of Thomas's own answers for all the remaining articles.

I have not added section headings and subheadings of my own. The question and article titles are those of the *Summa Theologica* itself.[1] Further, in this chapter I have retained the use of italics for direct quotations from Scripture and other sources as they appear italicized in the English Dominican translation.

Now, let's let St. Thomas show what Jerusalem has made of Athens as he examines Aristotelian friendship in the light of Christian charity.

ST, II-II, Q. 23. Of Charity Considered in Itself (Eight Articles)

1. Whether Charity is Friendship?

Thomas begins his analysis of the Christian theological virtue of charity by proposing three objections to his thesis that charity *is* friendship. All three objections cite statements in chapter 8 of Aristotle's *Nicomachean Ethics,* and the Scriptures are also referenced. The first objection holds that charity is not friendship, because friends dwell together and man's charity is directed to God and the angels who do not dwell with men.[2] The second holds that the love of friendship is reciprocal, while charity extends even to enemies

---

1. My main source has for years been St. Thomas Aquinas, *Summa Theologica,* Complete English edition in five volumes translated by Fathers of the English Dominican Province (Notre Dame, IN: Christian Classics [1911], 1981). I also use the *Summa Theologiae,* Latin/English Edition in eight volumes, featuring an updated version of the English Dominican Province translation (Lander, WY: The Aquinas Institute, 2012). Readers are also directed to the free online English edition at www.newadvent.org/summa. It, too, uses the English Dominican translation.

2. Dan. 2:11.

who do not return our love.[3] The third, citing Aristotle's theory of three kinds of friendship based on pleasure, use, or virtue, notes that charity is not friendship for pleasure or use. St. Jerome makes this clear when he writes that true friendship is not for sensual pleasure or the gains that come from crafty flattery, but is cemented together by Christ, the fear of God, and the joint study of Scriptures. Charity is not virtuous friendship, either, because virtuous friendship is reserved for virtuous men, while charity extends even to sinners.

Thomas answers to the contrary: "It is written (John 15:15) *I will not now call you servants . . . but My friends.* Now this was said to them by reason of nothing else than charity. Therefore charity is friendship." He writes that:

> According to the Philosopher (*Ethic* 8:2, 3), not every love has the character of friendship, but that love which is together with benevolence, when, to wit, we love someone so as to wish good to him. If, however, we do not wish good to what we love, but wish its good for ourselves, (thus we are said to love wine, or a horse, or the like), it is not love of friendship, but of a kind of concupiscence. For it would be absurd to speak of having friendship for wine or for a horse.
>
> Yet neither does well-wishing suffice for friendship, for a certain mutual love is requisite, since friendship is between friend and friend: and this well-wishing is founded on some kind of communication.
>
> Accordingly, since there is a communication between man and God, inasmuch as He communicates His happiness to us, some kind of friendship must needs be based on this same communication, of which it is written (1 Cor. 1:9): *God is faithful: by Whom you are called unto the fellowship of His Son.* The love which is based on this communication, is charity: wherefore it is evident that charity is the friendship of man for God.

Thomas then responds to each objection.

First, human life is twofold. We have a bodily and a spiritual nature. While we do not dwell with God and the angels bodily in

---

3. Matt. 5:44.

our present state on earth, in our spiritual life we do dwell and converse with them, though imperfectly, "as it is written (Phil. 3:20): *Our conversation is in heaven.* But this conversation will be perfected in heaven, when *His servants shall serve Him, and they shall see His face* (Apoc. 22:3, 4). Therefore, charity is imperfect here, but will be perfected in heaven."

Secondly, friendship extends to people in two ways, first directly to the friend himself, and secondly, indirectly to others who are loved by one's friend, such as his children or servants. It is in this way that the friendship of charity reaches even to our enemies. We love them out of charity in relation to God, Who is the direct object of our friendship.

Finally, building on the same point, while friendship is principally and directly shared only between virtuous people, for the virtuous friend's sake we also love those who belong to him, even if they are not virtuous. "In this way charity, which above all is friendship based on the virtuous, extends to sinners, whom, out of charity, we love for God's sake."

2. Whether Charity is Something Created in the Soul?

Here Thomas addresses the idea that, since God is Love and God is a Spirit, charity is not something created in the soul by God, but is the Holy Spirit Himself dwelling in the human mind. Thomas agrees with The Master (Augustine) when he states "(*On Christian Doctrine* 3:10): *By charity I mean the movement of the soul towards the enjoyment of God for His own sake,*" but he makes clear that movement in the soul is something created in the soul by the Holy Spirit, not the Holy Spirit Himself. The Holy Spirit moves the human will to the act of love, but the will cooperates and is itself the efficient cause by which acts of love are performed. The love of charity through which we love our neighbor is a participation in Divine charity. As God gives life to the soul by charity and life to the body by the soul, we may conclude that "just as the soul is immediately united to the body, so is charity to the soul."

3. Whether Charity is a Virtue?

Friendship is not a virtue in and of itself, as we see in the case of friendships based on pleasure or utility, but is, as The Philosopher (*Ethic* 8) notes, something consequent to a virtue in friendships of the virtuous. Charity, however, is in itself a virtue, one that orders our affections and unites us to God by its love. Charity is not based principally on human virtue, but on the goodness of God.

4. Whether Charity is a Special Virtue?

Charity is a special or particular virtue and not a general name for virtue, for St. Paul enumerates it in the same list as hope and faith: "1 Cor. 13:13: *And now there remain faith, hope, charity, these three.*" Therefore, charity is a special virtue. In the same way that the moral virtues of justice, fortitude, and temperance depend on the virtue of prudence or practical wisdom because it guides them, every virtue depends on charity for guidance. Also, all precepts or commandments from God not only follow the precept of love as a general command, but are reduced to it as their end, "according to Timothy 1:5: *The end of the commandment is charity.*"

5. Whether Charity is One Virtue?

It might seem that charity is not one virtue because it is directed to two objects, God and neighbor, which are an infinite distance from one another. This is not true. Charity is a kind of friendship of man for God, but it cannot be differentiated, as human friendships can, into those that seek the ends of pleasure, usefulness, or virtue, because its *one end* is the goodness of God. God is the principal object of charity, and we love our neighbor out of charity for God's sake.

6. Whether Charity is the Most Excellent of the Virtues?

It might seem that charity is not the highest of the virtues, because it resides in the *will* through which we love, while the *intellect* is higher than the will and directs it. Therefore, it would seem that faith, which resides in the intellect, is superior to charity. "*On the contrary,* It is written (1 Cor. 13:13): *The greater of these is charity.*" The human moral and intellectual virtues follow the rule of reason, while the theological virtues of faith, hope, and charity follow the rule of God, Who regulates even human reason. Hence, the theological virtues are the highest virtues, and among them the highest is the virtue that most closely attains God. While faith and hope attain God by means of the knowledge of truth or the acquisition of good, charity attains and rests in God Himself, not in what it might attain from him. Also, while things that are less excellent than the soul are more excellent when held in the soul than they are in themselves, things more excellent than the soul are better in themselves than they are as contained in the soul. Hence, while it is better to know than to love lesser things, it is better to love than to know things that are above us, especially God.

7. Whether Any True Virtue is Possible without Charity?

True virtue is directed at man's principal end of the enjoyment of God, "according to Ps. 73 [72]:28: *It is good for me to adhere to God.*" "The Philosopher says (*Physics* 7:17) that *virtue is the disposition of a perfect thing to that which is best.*" Therefore, while good acts can be performed to achieve particular ends without charity, no true virtue is possible without charity. Such acts without charity can be generically good, but not *perfectly* good, because they are not ordered to the highest, final end of the enjoyment of God.

8. Whether Charity is the Form of the Virtues?

Charity directs all the other virtues to the highest end of the enjoyment of God. In that sense, it gives form to all other virtuous actions. It is the end of the other virtues, because it directs them all to its own end. Since a mother conceives within herself by the action of another, charity is also called the mother of the virtues, because, in commanding them, it gives birth to the acts of the other virtues in desire of the last end.

Question 24: Of the Subject of Charity
(In Twelve Articles)

1. Whether the Will is the Subject of Charity?

The human will seeks the good as directed by the intellect. Charity also has the good as its object. Its object is the Divine Good which cannot be apprehended by the sense, but only by the intellect. "Therefore, charity is in the will as its subject."

2. Whether Charity is Caused in Us by Infusion?

"The Apostle says (Rom. 5:5): *The charity of God is poured forth in our hearts by the Holy Ghost, Who is given to us.*" Charity is a friendship of man for God, founded upon everlasting happiness. We cannot obtain eternal life by our own natural powers, but only by God's grace. We obtain charity "by the infusion of the Holy Ghost, Who is the love of the Father and the Son and the participation of Whom in us is created charity."

3. Whether Charity is Infused According to the Capacity of Our Natural Gifts?

John 3:8 writes: "*The Spirit breatheth where he will,*" and Paul (1 Cor. 12:11) writes: "*All these things one and the same Spirit worketh, dividing to every one according as He will.*" Therefore, our natural capacities for virtue do not determine the infusion of charity in us. It is purely a grace of God, distributed as He wills.

4. Whether Charity Can Increase?

It might seem that charity cannot increase, because it is does not have quantity or because it is already an extreme in itself. Following Augustine, Thomas concludes that charity does increase among "wayfarers" on earth as the affections of our soul move closer to God, the final end of our happiness. Charity increases, not in quantity, but in the intensity of its act, whereby a thing is loved more; in this way, it increases in virtual, not actual, quantity. Further, "charity is essentially a virtue ordained to act, so that an essential increase in charity implies ability to produce an act of more fervent love."

5. Whether Charity Increases by Addition?

Charity does not increase by God infusing in us additional quantities of it, but by ourselves partaking more and more of the charity He gives. Further, "charity increases by being intensified in its subject, and this is for charity an increase in its essence; and not by charity being added to charity."

6. Whether Charity Increases through Every Act of Charity?

Not every act of charity causes an increase in charity in us. If a charitable act is done reluctantly or half-heartedly, it could actually dispose us to a lower degree of charity. Rather, each charitable act disposes us to an increase in charity, in that such acts makes us more ready to act charitably again, "and this readiness increasing, man breaks out into an act of more fervent love, and strives to advance in charity, and then his charity increases actually."

7. Whether Charity Increases Indefinitely?

Charity can increase indefinitely throughout our life on earth because it is a participation in the infinite charity of the Holy Spirit, because God, charity's cause, is of infinite power, and because whenever charity increases, there is a corresponding growth in readiness for further increase. The potential for charity's growth is limitless in this life.

8. Whether Charity Can be Perfected in This Life?

Charity is perfected in this life by those who, like St. Paul, desire "to be dissolved and to be with Christ"—that is, who habitually give their time and their whole hearts to God, neither thinking about nor desiring anything contrary to the love of God. Charity in heaven is higher still, because there the heart is with God always.

9. Whether Charity is Rightly Distinguished into Three Degrees, Beginning, Progress, and Perfection?

Charity, Thomas tells us, increases in a way analogous to growth in human development, from the incapacities of infancy to the manifold powers of full maturity. Its growth can be seen in three stages or degrees of perfection.

> 1. *Beginners* are infants in the spirit, and their focus is primarily on *the avoidance of sin,* battling urges of the myriad of earthly desires that remove our hearts and minds from God.
>
> 2. *Proficients,* those at the second degree of development of charity, are consumed in the *pursuit of virtue*: "In second place, man's chief pursuit it to aim at progress in good, and this is the pursuit of the proficient, whose chief aim is to strengthen their charity, by adding to it." Although pursuing virtue is a noble and efficacious means of squelching sin, proficients must continue to fight the

good fight against their sinful natures. Thomas graphically compares this task to those who built the walls of Jerusalem while fighting off their enemies, who "with one hand labored on the work and with the other held up his weapon" (Neh. 4:17).

3. The *perfect* "aim chiefly at union with and enjoyment of God," and "*desire to be dissolved and to be with Christ.*"[4]

10. Whether Charity Can Decrease?

Virtues acquired through acts can decrease or cease altogether if those acts cease. This is why the Philosopher has noted in *Ethics* 8:5 that many friendships have been destroyed by a lack of interaction. Things are kept in being by their causes, and human virtues are caused by acts. Charity, however, is caused only by God. We do not have to act through our free-will to sustain charity, for it remains in us even while we sleep. Charity can only be decreased by God or by a gravely sinful act that prompts the removal of his grace. God does not turn away from man, but man may turn away from God.

11. Whether We Can Lose Charity Once We Have It?

We read in Revelation 2:4, "*But I have this against you, that you have abandoned the love you had at first.*"[5] The charity we possess on earth is changeable because of our imperfect free-will, which is not always directed toward God and can choose evil. The charity that the blessed possess in heaven sees God in His Essence, which is the very essence of goodness and can never be lost.

12. Whether Charity is Lost Through One Mortal Sin?

St. Paul has written that "*the wages of sin is death*" (Rom. 5:23), while those who have charity deserve eternal life: "*He that loveth Me, shall be loved by My Father, and I will love Him, and will manifest myself to him*" (John 14:21). Eternal life consists of this manifestation: "*This is eternal life; that they may know Thee, the . . . true God, and Jesus Christ Whom Thou hast sent.*" Since it would be a contradiction to be

---

4. It is reported that Christ once appeared to St. Thomas, telling him that he had written well and asking him what reward he would like. The Angelic Doctor's perfect answer was "*Non nisi te, Domine*"—"Only you, Lord."

5. RSV edition.

worthy at the same time of death and of eternal life, it is clear that charity is destroyed by mortal sin. In mortal sin, we act directly against the love of God. Just as the light in the air would instantly become dark if some obstacle blocked the sun, charity ceases at once in the soul once mortal sin blocks God's outpouring of charity. Through mortal sin, man places greater value on sin than he does on his friendship with God. Such friendship entails that he should follow God's will.

Question 25: Of the Object of Charity
(In Twelve Articles)

1. Whether the Love of Charity Stops at God, or Extends to Our Neighbor?

St. Thomas answers with the words of 1 John 4:21: "*This commandment we have from God, that he who loveth God also love his brother.*" Just as we see light, and also the color under the aspect of the light, by the same visual act, so too, by the spiritual act by which we love God, we also love our neighbor. We should love our neighbor under the aspect of God, that is, "what we ought to love in our neighbor is that he may be in God."

2. Whether We Should Love Charity out of Charity?

Augustine has written in *On the Trinity* 8:8, "*He that loves his neighbor, must, in consequence, love love itself,*" and since we love our neighbor out of charity, we also love charity out of charity. Charity, though, is not only love, but also has the nature of friendship. In friendship we love a thing in two ways: first, we love the friend and wish him good things, and secondly, we love the good we wish for the friend. It is in this second way that we love charity out of charity, because charity is that good which we wish him. "Charity is itself the fellowship of the spiritual life, whereby we arrive at happiness."

3. Whether Irrational Creatures Also Ought to be Loved out of Charity?

The love of charity is a kind of friendship, and we cannot wish to irrational creatures the goods that come from free choice; animals do not have the faculty of free choice, and we cannot share in conversation and fellowship with creatures unable to reason. Still, we may love irrational creatures out of charity if we consider them among the good things that we wish for others, thereby desiring that they are preserved to God's honor and man's use. In that sense, God also loves them out of charity.

4. Whether a Man Ought to Love Himself out of Charity?

"It is written (Levit. 14:18): *Thou shalt love thy friend as thyself.*" Considering charity under the notion of friendship, man is not a friend to himself, but something even more. Love unites different things, and a man is one with himself, which is more than being united with something else. Still, as unity is the principle of union, so is the love a man has for himself "the form and root of friendship." As noted in the *Nicomachean Ethics* 4:8, "*the origin of friendly relations with others lies in our relations to ourselves.*" We may also look at charity in its specific nature as man's friendship, primarily with God, and secondarily with the things of God, among which is the man himself. In that second sense, a man does love himself out of charity.

5. Whether a Man Ought to Love His Body out of Charity?

We should love our own bodies out of charity. What God has made is good, and we may use our bodies "*as instruments of justice unto God*" per Rom. 6:13. Although our bodies cannot know and love God, it is by the works of our bodies that we are able to come to know God. "Hence from the enjoyment in the soul there overflows a certain happiness into the body," and since the body has a share of this happiness, it can be loved with charity.

6. Whether We Ought to Love Sinners out of Charity?

As Augustine has noted, we have been instructed to love our neighbor, and we should consider every person, including the sinner, as our neighbor. We love the sinner in his *nature*, which is good and from God, but we hate his *guilt*, whereby he opposes God. It is our duty to hate the sin of the sinner, but to love the sinner himself, since he is a man capable of bliss, "and this is to love him truly, out of charity, for God's sake."

7. Whether Sinners Love Themselves?

"It is written (Ps. 10:6): *He that loveth iniquity, hateth his own soul.*" There is a kind of love of self that all share, a kind that is common only among the good, and a kind that is common only among the wicked. All men love their own preservation. Good men look at their rational natures, the "inward man" per 2 Cor. 4:16, as of prime importance in determining what they are. Wicked men, on the contrary, consider their sensitive and bodily nature, the "outward man," as defining what they are. In this, the wicked do not truly know themselves and do not truly love themselves. The Philosopher proves this from the five things that true friends desire and do for their friends:

1. A friend desires his friend to be, to exist.

2. A friend desires good things for his friend.

3. A friend does good deeds for his friend.

4. A friend takes pleasure in his friend's company.

5. A friend is of one mind with his friend, rejoicing and sorrowing in almost the same things.

The true friend then desires the spiritual goods of the "inward man" for his friend, and their wills do not conflict, since they desire the same things. The wicked, on the contrary, do not preserve the integrity of the "inward man" and wish spiritual goods for themselves, they do not work toward that end, and they do not take pleasure in their own company, because when they examine their own hearts, what they find there of the past, present, and future is evil and base. Further, they do not even agree with themselves, because of "the gnawings of conscience according to Ps. 50:21: *I will reprove thee and set before thy face.*" The wicked love themselves according to the corruption of the "outward man," but their self-love is not true, but only apparent, since they think themselves good when they are not.

8. Whether Charity Requires That We Should Love Our Enemies?

Our Lord said: "*Love your enemies*" (Matt. 5:44). We do not love our enemies *because* they are opposed to us, but because of their nature, in which they are included among our neighbors. Charity does not require that we perform specific acts of love for every man, but that we should be prepared to act out of love toward every individual enemy if some necessity would require it. If a man should actually perform some act of love toward his enemy for God's sake in situations where it is not necessary, his act bespeaks the perfection of charity. The more man loves God, the more he puts enmities aside and shows love toward all neighbors, as when, for example, because of our deep love for a friend, we also love his children, even if they are unfriendly toward us.

9. Whether It is Necessary for Salvation That We Should Show Our Enemies the Signs and Effects of Love?

As discussed in the previous article, charity requires that we should inwardly love our enemies in general, but not individually. We should, for example, pray for our enemies, but we are not required to show the same signs and effects of love to our enemies as we would to our friends. We should always be ready to come to an enemy's aid in an emergency, however, as is written in Proverbs 25:21: "*If thy enemy be hungry, give him to eat; if he thirst, give him . . . drink.*" We are not obliged to do more outside of emergencies, but to do so is a perfection of charity whereby we wish to overcome evil by good.

10. Whether We Ought to Love the Angels out of Charity?

The friendship of charity is founded upon the fellowship of everlasting happiness, which men have in common with the angels, for it is written that "*in the resurrection . . . men shall be as the angels of God in heaven*" (Matt. 22:30). The friendship of charity, then, extends to angels.

11. Whether We Out to Love the Demons out of Charity?

"It is written (Isaiah 28:18): *Your league with death shall be abolished, and your covenant with hell shall not stand.*" Peace and covenants are perfected through charity, so that we should not extend charity to the demons of hell who compass death. We are to love the nature of a sinner, but not his sin, and the demons have deformed their very natures through their choice of sin. We cannot extend friendship to demons, wishing them good, when God has condemned them eternally, for this would oppose our charity toward God and approval of His justice.

12. Whether Four Things are Rightly Reckoned as to be Loved out of Charity, viz. God, Our Neighbor, Our Body and Ourselves?

Augustine wrote in *On Christian Doctrine* 1:23 that of the four things we love, one is above us (God), one is ourselves, another beside us (our neighbor), and a third is below us (our own body). The friendship of charity is based on the fellowship of happiness. God is lovable as the source from which this happiness flows, and men and angels as partakers in that happiness. Even the body is lovable, because happiness comes as an overflow into the human body.

Question 26: Of the Order of Charity
(In Thirteen Articles)

1. Whether There is Order in Charity?

The love of charity is unique among the virtues in that it tends to God as the source of happiness, the last end, and the First Principle. There is an order of things that are to be loved in regard to God as the first principle of love, and all the other virtues follow the order dictated by charity.

2. Whether God Ought to be Loved More Than Our Neighbor?

God should be loved foremost, out of charity, because he is the source of happiness, whereas our neighbor shares with us in that happiness God has provided.

3. Whether, out of Charity, Man is Bound to Love God More Than Himself?

By the nature God has given us, we love and seek to preserve our individual lives, but we love even more the common good, as is seen when citizens sometimes give up their own property for the sake of the common good. The friendship of charity is founded, however, not merely upon nature, but upon the fellowship of the gifts of the graces of God. Therefore, charity should prompt a man to love God even more than himself, since God is the fountain and source of happiness for himself and for all.

4. Whether out of Charity, Man Ought to Love Himself More Than His Neighbor?

That we are to love our neighbors as ourselves (Lev. 19:18; Matt. 22:39) implies that love of self is the model of love for others, and as models are more excellent than their copies, so too is love of self more excellent than love of neighbor. This love of self refers only to man's spiritual nature, not his bodily nature. A man should not commit a sin that would harm his own soul, even for the sake of his neighbor. He should, however, be willing to suffer bodily injury for the sake of his friend. This perfects the virtue of the man's spiritual mind.

5. Whether a Man Ought to Love His Neighbor More Than His Own Body?

Thomas agrees with Augustine, who writes (*On Christian Doctrine* 1:27) that *"we ought to love our neighbor more than our own body."* While our body is nearer to our soul than our neighbor, our neighbor is closer to our soul in terms of the participation of happiness that comes from fellowship in charity, while the body, as previously noted, participates only secondarily by way of overflow.

6. Whether We Ought to Love One Neighbor More Than Another?

We should love some neighbors more than others. It is a more grievous sin to act against the love of some neighbors, for example, in Leviticus 20:9: *"He that curseth his father, or mother, dying let him die."* We love all men equally in that we wish all the same good of everlasting happiness, but we love some neighbors more intensely than others, depending on how closely they are related to God. Some are closer to God because of their greater goodness, and these we should love more than those who are not near to God.

7. Whether We Ought to Love Those Who are Better More Than Those Who are More Closely United to Us?

It is written (1 Tim. 5:8): "*If any man have not care of his own, and especially of those of his house, he hath denied the faith, and is worse than an infidel.*" Acts should be proportionate to both their objects and their agents. The *object* of charity's love is *God*, while *man* is the loving *agent*. In regard to the object of charity, we should wish a greater good to those who are closest to God. In terms of the intensity of love within us, we love those who are most intimately related to us with the greatest affection. We more strongly desire that goods be granted to them, while we wish that others closer to God attain even greater goods. When we share closer bonds of kinship and virtuous friendship with those who are near to us, we share the love of charity in more ways than we do with those who are farther removed.

8. Whether We Ought to Love More Those Who are Connected with Us by Ties of Blood?

As we can see from the fourth commandment of the Decalogue (Exodus 20:12), we are especially obliged to honor our parents. Therefore, we should love more specially those who are most closely related to us. The intensity of our love should reflect the closeness of our union.

9. Whether a Man Ought, out of Charity, to Love His Children More Than His Father?

"Ambrose says: *We ought to love God first, then our parents, then our children, and lastly those of our household.*" From the standpoint of love's object, the better and more like God a thing is, the more it should be loved, and hence, a man should love his father more than his children, because his father is his principle, and is, in that sense, a higher good and more like God. From the standpoint of the lover, a man loves what is more closely related to him, and in this way, he loves his children more, since children are parts of the parents, while a father is not part of his son. Thomas includes other reasons, including a fourth: that parents have loved longer, since they love their child immediately, while the child does not do so until it has developed. Children owe their parents primarily honor, while parents owe their children primarily care.

10. Whether a Man Ought to Love His Mother More Than His Father?

Thomas cites Jerome, who wrote, commenting on Ezekiel 44:25, that we should first love God as Father, then our father, and then our mother, who is mentioned last. Thomas acknowledges that the father and mother may differ in virtue in ways that can diminish our friendship with either of them, but he argues that, strictly speaking, we should love our father as father more than our mother as mother. While both are principles of our natural origin, the father is the more excellent active principle, while the mother is the passive, material principle.[6]

11. Whether a Man Ought to Love His Wife More Than His Father and Mother?

Ephesians 5:28 indicates that *"men ought to love their wives as their own bodies."* We saw above (article 5) that we ought to love our bodies less than our neighbor, and among all neighbors parents are those most worthy of love. Therefore, a man should love his parents more than his wife as the objects of his love, but in terms of the marital union in which man and wife become one flesh as per Matt. 19:6, his wife should be loved more. "Consequently," Thomas concludes, "a man loves his wife more intensely, but his parents with greater reverence."

12. Whether a Man Ought to Love More His Benefactor Than One He has Benefited?

Thomas stands with The Philosopher (*Ethic* 9:7) when he wrote that *"benefactors seem to love recipients of their benefactions, rather than*

---

6. This example relies upon the dated biological understanding of his time. Thomas sometimes uses examples based on the science of his day, and has written of his awareness that such scientific understandings may change as additional knowledge is acquired.

vice versa." Considering that things are loved in two ways, we should love the benefactor as a more excellent object of love, being the principle of good to the person he benefits, while, from the perspective of the lover, we love those who receive benefits in four ways:

1. they are, in a sense, the handiwork resulting from our benefits, and a person loves his own work,

2. we see our virtuous good manifested in the receiver of the benefits,

3. it is the lover's part to will and act, as does the benefactor, while the recipient is passive, and

4. it is more difficult to give favors than to receive them, and we are more fond of things that require great effort, while we almost despise what is too easy for us.

13. Whether the Order of Charity Endures in Heaven?

The ways and order of nature will not be eliminated, but perfected in the state of eternal glory. The order of charity will therefore remain in heaven. Man will love God above all things, and all things else to the degree that they conform to God's Divine will. In this sense, he will love better men more than himself and lesser men less than himself. Yet in the second sense of love, from the perspective of the lover as agent, man will love himself more intensely even than better men.

Question 27: Of the Principal Act of Charity, Which is to Love (In Eight Articles)

1. Whether to be Loved is More Proper to Charity Than to Love?

Charity is a virtue and therefore has an inclination toward its proper act, which is to love rather than to be loved. We see that friends are praised more for loving than for being loved, and that if a friend is loved and does not love back, it is blameworthy. Further, as The Philosopher has noted (*Ethic* 8:8), the greatest love is that of a mother, who seeks to love rather than to be loved.

2. Whether to Love Considered as an Act of Charity is the Same as Goodwill?

Goodwill, that act of the will whereby we wish another well, is, as The Philosopher notes (*Ethic* 9:5) the beginning of friendship, but the love that denotes an affective union between the lover and the beloved is also required. The love of charity, then, includes not only goodwill but the desire for intimate union.

3. Whether Out of Charity God Ought to be Loved for Himself?

Thomas agrees with Augustine (*On Christian Doctrine*, 1), who notes that to enjoy something is to cleave to something for its own sake, and who writes in the same book that we are to enjoy God. We can love God for something other than Himself, such as the favors that He grants us, the future rewards we hope for in Him, or even the punishments that we are reminded to avoid through Him. Yet principally we are to love God for his own sake, because he is the final cause, the ultimate end, and every other thing is good only insofar as it partakes of His substance.

4. Whether God can be Loved Immediately in This Life?

While our knowledge of God on earth comes to us through other things, as effects lead back to knowledge of their cause, our love of God is immediate and direct even while on earth, because the love of charity tends to God first and flows on from Him to other creatures.

5. Whether God can be Loved Wholly?

Though it might seem that we cannot love God wholly, because love follows knowledge and we do not know God wholly, we are commanded to love God with all our heart (Deut. 6:5). To love God wholly can be understood in three ways:

1. When *wholly* refers to the thing loved, we should love God wholly, including all that pertains to God.

2. When *wholly* to refers to the lover, we, again, should love God wholly, with all our might, as instructed in Deuteronomy.

3. When *wholly* refers to the comparison of the lover to the thing loved, in that sense we cannot love God wholly, since things are loved in proportion to their goodness and God is infinitely good and lovable. No creature can love God infinitely, for all of its love, whether natural or infused by God, is finite.

6. Whether in Loving God We Ought to Observe Any Mode?

St. Bernard says in *On Loving God*, ch. 1, that *"God is the cause of our loving God; the measure is to love Him without measure."* The Philosopher writes in *Politics* 1:3, *"in every art, the desire for the end is endless and unlimited."* Because the ultimate end of all human actions is the love of God, there is no mode or proper mean between loving too much or too little, since love itself is the measure. There can be no excess of love of God, and "the more we love God the better our love is."

7. Whether It is More Meritorious to Love an Enemy Than to Love a Friend?

"It would seem more meritorious to love an enemy than to love a friend. For it is written (Matt. 5:46): *If you love them that love you, what reward shall you have? . . .* [Yet] the better an action is, the more meritorious it is. Now … it is better to love a better man, and the friend who loves you is better than the enemy who hates you. Therefore, it is more meritorious to love one's friend than to love one's enemy." There is a second way in which the love of an enemy is better; a friend may be loved for some reason beside the sake of God, "whereas God is the only reason for loving one's enemy." The love of charity can be compared to the power of a furnace; the stronger the furnace, the further out it will throw its heat. If the love of our charity extends even to enemies, it attests to the power of the furnace of our love. However, just as a fire produces the most heat for what is nearest to it, so, too, should our love of charity burn with greatest fervor for those united to us, rather than those who are farthest away. In this sense, the love of friends is more intense and fervent than the love of neighbors.

As for Our Lord's words in Matthew 5, if we love our friends merely because they are our friends and do not love them for God's sake, out of the love of charity, then such love is not meritorious. If we do love our friends for God's sake, it is meritorious for that reason, and not merely because they are our friends.

8. Whether It is More Meritorious to Love One's Neighbor Than to Love God?

As noted above, the love of neighbor is not meritorious unless the neighbor is loved for God's sake. Therefore, the love of God is more meritorious than the love of neighbor. We may consider this first by looking at both loves separately. The love of God is more meritorious because that love is rewarded for its own sake: "(John 14:21): *He that loveth Me, shall be loved of My Father, and I will . . . manifest myself to him.*" Love of neighbor includes love of God, while the love of God stands alone without love of neighbor. Hence, the love of God is perfect, and the love of neighbor is inadequate and imperfect on its own, for "this commandment we have from God, that he who loveth God, love also his brother (1 John 4:21)."

8

Aquinas's Theocentric
Legacy of *Caritas* as *Amicitia*

It is certainly right to observe that St. Thomas's entire theological
project, like that of Aelred, is fundamentally driven by the desire
for God.

~Nathan Lefler, *Theologizing Friendship*[1]

As we saw from the samples in our last chapter, St. Thomas's writings on friendship in relationship to Christian charity, though broad and deep, are easily understood. In this chapter I will provide a little background in terms of St. Thomas's sources and then highlight a few key ideas regarding what I will call his "charitable friendship," drawing from Thomas's metaphor of the growth of a tree. The last section will address the legacy of St. Thomas's writings on friendship even unto our day.

The Root of Charitable Friendship

What did St. Thomas consider the "root" of friendship? We know, because he told us explicitly: "just as unity is the principle of union, the love with which a man loves himself is the form and root of friendship" (ST, II-II, Q. 25, a.4). *Self-love*, then, is the root of friendship. But what exactly does he mean by a "root"?

Elsewhere in the *Summa Theologica*, (I-II, Q. 84, a. 1), expound-

---

1. Nathan Lefler, *Theologizing Friendship: How Amicitia in the Thought of Aelred and Aquinas Inscribes the Scholastic Turn* (Eugene, OR: Pickwick Publications, 2014), 155.

ing upon the meaning of the word "root" in 1 Tim. 6:10—"The desire of money is the root of all evil"—Thomas explains that, in the same way that the root provides sustenance to the whole tree, money serves as the means to satisfy all kinds of worldly desires for the greedy man. Self-love, then, is that which provides sustenance to the tree of friendship.

Self-love makes a striking appearance elsewhere in the *Summa Theologica* (I-II, Q. 77, a. 4): "It is evident that inordinate self-love is the cause of every sin." Of course, the key word is "inordinate." In his treatment of the causes of sin, Thomas expounds that such inordinate self-love produces contempt for God. While he notes there that "well ordered self-love, whereby man desires a fitting good for himself, is right and natural," it is in his examination of charity that he demonstrates how ordinate, proper, or fitting self-love is indeed the root of friendship.

St. Thomas's understanding of self-love, friendship, and charity had, in a sense, two deep and sturdy root systems. In our last chapter's summary of Question 23, article 1—his first article on charity—we saw that his first and deepest root system is derived from Scripture, and, indeed, from Christ Himself. His "On the contrary" section immediately cites Christ's words in John 15:15: "*I will not now call you servants ... but My friends.*" As for his second source, his "I answer that" section immediately expounds upon Aristotle's *Nicomachean Ethics,* 8:2–3, in which he explains the kind of love that is unique to friendship. As we move through St. Thomas's examination of friendship, we soon find additional roots that have sprouted from God's Word in the writings of the Church Fathers, most notable among them being St. Augustine. While Aelred openly declared his debt to Cicero's account of friendship, but lamented how unpalatable it had become without the name of Christ, Thomas deftly weaves Aristotle's writings into his own Christian arguments as if they are spun of the same cloth.

From Aristotle, Thomas concludes that self-love is the "root" and "form" of friendship, citing *Nicomachean Ethics,* 9: "*the origin of friendly relations with others lies in our relations to ourselves.*" Characteristically, even before this elaboration he has cited a scriptural foundation: "It is written (Levit. 19:18): *Thou shalt love thy friend as thyself.*" Thomas then elaborates upon Aristotle's description of what appropriate self-love is: love of our higher nature and the perfection of our reason, rather than the inordinate self-love that seeks merely to serve our sensitive, animal wants and needs. Further, Thomas declares that love of self is our model of love for others, and, as models are more excellent than their copies, in that sense appropriate love of self is more excellent even than the love of neighbor.

When Thomas, in II-II, Q.25, a.7, declares that sinners do not truly love themselves—expounding upon Psalm 10:6: "*He that loveth iniquity, hateth his own soul*"—he draws from Aristotle's insight that the five things proper to friendship are what build upon a man's appropriate self-love.[2] Sadly, an inveterate sinner is not really a friend to himself.

Thomas goes on to address a number of potential "objects" of charity, including God, neighbor, animals (only in a qualified sense, lacking reason), our bodies, sinners, enemies, angels, demons (not proper objects because they chose to deform their very natures by sin), and even charity itself. All of these possible forms of charity are grounded and nourished by the root that is proper self-love, which honors the faculties of intellect and will whereby we were made in God's image.

The Trunk of Charitable Friendship

Self-love is the root and form of friendship, because it is from the experience of unity within ourselves that we can begin to reach out to and join with second selves. It is the acorn to the oak of fully-grown friendship, but what constitutes the trunk? St. Thomas does not use the trunk metaphor, but his colleague, St. Bonaventure, in speaking of the Holy Spirit's gift of fear of the Lord, has used an arboreal metaphor that has some relevance here:

---

2. To recap: 1. A friend desires his friend to be, to exist. 2. A friend desires good things for his friend. 3. A friend does good deeds for his friend. 4. A friend takes pleasure in his friend's company. 5. A friend is of one mind with his friend, rejoicing and sorrowing in almost the same things.

It seems to me that the fear of the Lord is a very beautiful tree planted in the heart of the holy person and watered continuously by God. And when that tree has grown to its fullness, that person is worthy of eternal life.[3]

The gift of fear of the Lord is one of seven "spirits" enumerated in Isaiah 11:2–3 that were prophesied to be given most fully to the Savior, Jesus Christ, through the action of the Holy Spirit. This gift has been characterized as beginning in a fear of punishment from God, known as *servile* fear. In perfected fear of the Lord, servile fear is replaced by a *filial* fear that dreads, not God's punishment, but the possibility that one will let down or disappoint God Himself by not living up to His expectations, as an adult child might fear to let down his parents, or as a married person might fear to let down a spouse. And what is it that perfects servile fear as it grows into filial fear? Scripture tells us that "there is no fear in love, but perfect love casts out fear. For fear has to do with punishment, and he who fears is not perfected in love. We love because he loved us" (1 John 18–19).

For St. Thomas, it is Christ Himself whose love has driven out servile fear. Indeed, the foundational verse of Thomas's treatise on charity as friendship with God builds on this same idea, presented in the words of Christ Himself: "No longer do I call you servants . . . but I have called you friends" (John 15:15). Christ has cast out servile fear by the love of friendship. *If natural self-love is the root of friendship, the trunk is the vertical beam of Christ's cross.* As Christ declared two verses before, "Greater love has no man than this, that a man lay down his life for his friends" (John 15:13).

Thus, while appropriate self-love is the root of friendship for St. Thomas much as it is for Aristotle, a difference between these writers arises in the matter of the trunk, or the heart, of true friendship. You may recall that Aristotle argued in book 8, chapter 7 that friendship between man and gods would be impossible because of the vast disparity in the nature of the two different kinds of selves. Elsewhere, he noted that men and gods do not live and converse

---

3. St. Bonaventure, *Collations on the Seven Gifts of the Holy Spirit*, Zachary Hayes, O.F.M. trans. (St. Bonaventure, NY: Franciscan Publications, 2008), 50.

together as do friends. St. Thomas writes about the one God who, three centuries after Aristotle's death, came down to dwell and to converse with men, making us his friends.

In a perceptive modern study of St. Thomas's writings on friendship, Daniel Schwartz examines extensively the notion of concord, harmony, or conformity in wills or opinions that Aristotle, Cicero, and Thomas all consider central to friendship.[4] While Cicero talks about harmony or accord "in all things," which might be seen to include opinions on important issues, Thomas—following Aristotle's *Nicomachean Ethics*, book 9, chapter 6—allows for significant differences in views or opinions between friends, as long as they share concordance in wills, that is, fundamental goals or goods of value to them both, though they may disagree as to means of attaining them. In his *Commentary on the Sentences of Peter Lombard*, Thomas discusses a dispute between angels, reported in Daniel 10:13, as evidence that disagreements about factual matters—in this case, the merits of the Jewish people at the time—are possible between friends bound in charity. What the angels had in common was the will that Divine Providence be fulfilled. Schwartz notes that the same principle would explain the legitimacy of differences in some opinions, but conformity of wills, in the friendships of such important Church Fathers as Sts. Augustine and Jerome.

We might ask how we can attain conformity with God's will when there is an infinite gap between God's knowledge and our own, such that even the angels cannot fully know God's will. Thomas notes elsewhere in the *Summa* that "a thing can be loved perfectly, even without being perfectly known" (I-II, Q. 27. a. 2).

We are to desire conformity of our will with God's, though it can never be complete. Yet Thomas has written extensively about the gifts of the Holy Spirit that make us disposed and more amenable to the stirrings of the Holy Spirit, these gifts that perfect our appetites, intellects, and wills being regulated not merely by human reason, but by the Holy Spirit Himself. In this way, God provides special aids to us his friends whereby we may more fully conform our will

4. Daniel Schwartz, *Aquinas on Friendship* (New York: Oxford University Press, 2007).

to His, as is seen on earth in the lives of the saints, who are true friends of God.

The Branches of Charitable Friendship

St. Catherine of Siena (1347–1380), a Dominican who was influenced by St. Thomas Aquinas,[5] used an arboreal metaphor in the spiritual writings of her *Dialogues.* She wrote that those mired in inappropriate self-love are diseased trees bearing rotten fruits, while the seven deadly sins[6] are seven branches drooping to the earth because only earthly things can feed them and they are never satisfied. Such are the branches that sprout from *inordinate* self-love, but what are the branches of the proper self-love that is fed and nourished by Christ?

If the vertical beam of Christ's cross represents the trunk of friendship that rises up to God, then the horizontal crossbeam is the branch that stretches out in love to reach the most distant of our neighbors, yet which provides that stoutest support to those who are closest to us within the bonds of kinship and friendship. After John wrote that perfect love casts off fear, he declared: "We love because he first loved us. If anyone says, 'I love God,' and hates his brother, he is a liar; for he who does not love his brother whom he has seen, cannot love God whom he has not seen. And this commandment we have from him, that he who loves God should love his neighbor also" (1 John 4:20–21).

We see especially in Questions 25–27, which deal with the objects, order, and love of charity, how St. Thomas meticulously spells out the implications of the great commandment of charity, to love God with all that we are, and our neighbors as ourselves (Lev. 19:18; Matt. 22:39). In Question 27, article 8, Thomas provides an illuminating and heartwarming analogy that helps us to distinguish the charity we should have for all from the special charity that we share

---

5. Her biographer, Blessed Raymond of Capua, notes that the uneducated Catherine was given the capacity to write at around the age of 30 in a mystical vision in which Christ was accompanied by St. John and St. Thomas Aquinas.

6. Pride, greed, envy, wrath, lust, gluttony, and sloth.

with close friends. He compares the love of charity to the heat of a powerful furnace. When our hearts burn with the fires of charity, their far-reaching flames will serve to warm strangers and even our enemies. But just as those closest to the furnace receive the most heat, true charity should be directed in greatest intensity to the Spirit who dwells within our hearts and to those who are nearest to us—our families and our friends.

In Question 24, article 6, Thomas explains that, while charity as a theological virtue is infused into our hearts by God, it may increase or decrease through our actions. With moving eloquence he tells us how each act of charity increases within us the disposition or tendency for more charitable acts, "and this readiness increasing, breaks out into an act of more fervent love, and strives to advance in charity, and then his charity increases actually" (*ST,* II-II, Q. 24, a.6).

Aristotle says that we become builders by building and harpists by playing the harp. So too, Thomas tells us, we become fervent lovers by loving fervently.

The Fruits of Charitable Friendship[7]

How will we know that we have forged fruitful friendships in which we love our neighbors as ourselves through our love for God? In Questions 28–33, Thomas explores, in a total of 34 articles, both the interior and exterior "effects which result from the principal act of charity, which is love" (II-II, 28, Prologue). Here are these fruits of the love of charity:

Interior Effects of Charity

1. *Joy*—We experience joy when we attain that which we love, and God is in those who love him "by his most excellent effect, according to John 4:16: *He that abideth in charity, abideth in God, and God in him.* Therefore, spiritual joy, which is about God, is caused by charity." (II-II, Q. 28, a.1.)

---

7. While Thomas called them *effecti* (effects) of charity, they are actually listed as "fruits" in the current *Catechism of the Catholic Church,* paragraph 1829.

2. *Peace*—The concord born of the love of charity between virtuous friends produces a twofold peace. The first is an internal peace experienced when one's own passions and appetites are directed toward the same aims, and second is the peace between friends when they seek the same things. When one directs his whole heart to God, his desires conform to the same things, and when we love our neighbor as ourselves, we desire to fulfill our neighbor's will as if it were our own.

3. *Mercy*—Mercy is a heartfelt sympathy for another's distress that impels us to comfort him. The Latin word for mercy, *misericordia*, itself refers to a compassionate heart (*miserum cor*). Aristotle notes that a friend "shares his friend's distress and enjoyment," in book 9, chapter 4 of the *Nicomachean Ethics*.[8] The Apostle Paul tells us, "*Rejoice with them that rejoice, weep with them that weep*" (Romans 12:15).

Exterior Effects of Charity

1. *Beneficence*—Thomas explains that beneficence simply means doing good for someone. It is an effect of the love of charity toward a friend when it arises from the benevolence (good will) through which a man wishes his friend well. It is essentially, good will in action.

2. *Almsdeeds*—Thomas does not refer only to giving money to those in need. He notes that *eleemosynarum* (translated as almsdeeds) has been defined as "*a deed whereby something is given to the needy, out of compassion and for God's sake.*" The scope of almsdeeds is very broad and is encapsulated in the Church's traditional seven corporal and spiritual acts of mercy, whereby we tend to our neighbor's physical and spiritual needs. The corporal acts of mercy were listed in Thomas's time as follows: feed the hungry, give drink to the thirsty, clothe the naked, harbor the homeless, visit the sick, ransom captives, and bury the dead. The spiritual acts of mercy were to instruct the ignorant, counsel the doubtful, comfort the sorrowful, reprove the sinner, forgive injuries, bear with those who annoy and trouble us, and to pray for all.[9] These

---

8. Irwin translation, 141.

9. The modern rendering of these lists, with minor variations from those in St. Thomas, may be found in the *Catechism of the Catholic Church*, paragraph 2447.

are acts motivated by mercy, as the Latin word *eleeymosynarum* derives from the Greek word *eleos* for mercy. Almsdeeds are mercy in action, and, as mercy is an effect of charity, "almsgiving is an act of charity through the medium of mercy" (II-II, Q.32, a.1).

3. *Fraternal correction*—Thomas states that in correcting wrong-doers to remedy their sins we act to spare from evil the sinner himself, to spare others whom may be harmed or scandalized by his sin, or even for the sake of preventing or repairing damage to the common good. Here, perhaps, we seen an application and extension of issues brought up by Aristotle and Cicero. Aristotle advised us to attempt to correct a friend who has fallen into vice before breaking off a friendship, and Cicero noted that we should neither ask of a friend nor do for a friend an evil act. In fraternal correction, we demonstrate care for the soul of our friend, as well as for those of all of our neighbors, by speaking out to turn a friend from sin.

Thomas, as he is wont to do, examines each of these effects of friendship in great detail and nuance. Such interior and exterior fruits of charity should be internally experienced and outwardly expressed to all of our neighbors, but most intensely and frequently to our closest friends. These fruits are well worth pondering today. To what extent do we experience joy, mercy, and peace through our friendships with God and neighbor? To what extent are we acting on these feelings? Thomas himself advises us, in one of my favorite of all of his sayings:

> Now the love of neighbor requires that not only should we be our neighbor's well-wishers, but also his well-doers, according to 1 John 3:18: *Let us not love in word, nor in tongue, but in deed, and in truth.*

The New Sprouts of Charitable Friendship

The voluminous works of Thomas Aquinas have, of course, had a massive legacy within the Catholic Church since his death on March 7, 1274. He is the Church's premiere theologian. His praises have been sung by dozens of popes and the modern *Catechism of the Catholic Church* is rich in citations from Thomas, even in his writings on charity as friendship. Thomas's impact has not only been felt in Catholic theology, but in philosophy. We mentioned earlier that modern social scientist Charles Murray has classified Aristotle as the world's most influential philosopher. Thomas Aquinas also made his list, coming in at number 6 among the "giants" of Western philosophy—ranking ahead of the likes of Socrates and Augustine. This is all the more impressive when we recall that philosophy was not Thomas's specialty, but merely a tool—a "handmaiden" to theology, the highest of all branches of learning. In a like manner, Thomas's writings on charity and friendship have had a wide audience within and outside of the Church. I will provide several very recent examples of works that have sprouted from Thomas's writings on friendship.

A great recent resource for philosophers is *Other Selves: Philosophers on Friendship,* an anthology of philosophical writings on friendship from one dozen key secular and religious thinkers throughout history.[10] Editor Michael Pakaluk chose to include several of Thomas's articles from questions 23–28 on charity as friendship in "the second part of the second part" of the *Summa Theologica,* essentially the same material that was summarized in this book. Pakaluk sums up his Introduction to Aquinas with the following insight on the centrality of charity and friendship to Thomas's entire moral philosophy and theology:

> Every human action without exception is done out of love, according to Aquinas (q. 28, a.6). Hence, if that love is charity—a kind of friendship—then friendship of a certain kind becomes the overarching and organizing virtue of one's entire moral life. This is indeed what we find in Aquinas's discussion of charity (II-II, q. 26). Moral action becomes nothing other than action that observes the proper order of charity, and this order depends upon two relations: the closeness of a person to oneself and the nearness of a person to God.[11]

---

10. Michael Pakaluk, ed., *Other Selves: Philosophers on Friendship* (Indianapolis, IN: Hackett Publishing Company, 1991).

11. Ibid., 148.

Daniel Schwartz's excellent book *Aquinas on Friendship* grew from his academic dissertation.[12] He provides an overview of Thomas's writings on friendship including and besides the *Summa Theologica*, and highlights in intriguing analyses the implications of concord and uniformity of wills in human friendships, friendship with God, and even friendship between angels. Schwartz notes that "for Aquinas, friendship is the paradigm ideal for the relationship that rational beings should cultivate," noting "the idea of friendship with God undoubtedly places considerable strain upon the conception of friendship that Aquinas inherited from Aristotle."[13]

Schwartz examines the way pride harms, destroys, or prevents friendship—with special attention to how pride and the related vice of vainglory impede a uniformity of wills—along with a fascinating analysis of how the virtue hope is essential to friendship, building, for example, upon this position of St. Thomas:

> So, to the extent that others help us, we come to see their own well-being as part of ours: 'In so far as hope regards one through whom something becomes possible to us, love is caused by hope, and not vice-versa. Because by the very fact that we hope that a good will accrue to us through someone, we are moved towards Him to our own good; and thus we begin to love him.[14]

My section in this chapter on "the root of friendship" was inspired not only by St. Thomas's own words, but by a recent book-length study, Anthony T. Flood's *The Root of Friendship: Self-Love and Self-Governance in Aquinas*.[15] This book highlights the interconnectedness of Thomas's thoughts on self-love as the basis for friendship and on how such proper self-love is central to a person's experience of self, as well as his ability to regulate the self in pursuit of happiness. Per Flood:

---

12. Daniel Schwartz, *Aquinas on Friendship* (New York: Oxford University Press, 2007).

13. Ibid., 1.

14. Ibid., 114, citing ST, I-II, Q. 40, a.7.

15. Anthony T. Flood, *The Root of Friendship: Self-Love and Self-Governance in Aquinas* (Washington, DC: Catholic University Press, 2014).

Self-love, particularly as fully actualized in self-friendship, constitutes a person's experience of himself, which in turn is the subjective pole for a person's ongoing experience of the world, including goods, and for acting in the world, particularly in terms of consciously responding to good.[16]

Flood proceeds to trace the implications of proper self-love as it pertains to issues including the understanding of personhood, natural law, the virtue of prudence or practical wisdom, and the hindering vice of pride (a vice, you might recall, that also made St. Aelred's list as a bane to friendship, and which is also addressed by Schwartz in the context of Aquinas's writings).

Like Schwartz's, Flood's book grew from an academic dissertation, as did a third, very recent book, Nathan Lefler's *Theologizing Friendship: How Amicitia in the Thought of Aelred and Aquinas Inscribes the Scholastic Turn*.[17] Lefler provides masterful summaries of both men's writings, including a perceptive analysis of Aelred's unique theology of "three Sabbaths," expounded in *The Mirror of Charity*, and how it relates to spiritual friendship.[18] He shows how the writings of Aelred and Thomas respectively personify the character and perfection of monastic and scholastic writing. He also confirms that, as far as we can tell, St. Thomas was not familiar with Aelred's writings. How intriguing it is to think what he might have made of them had he known them!

Perhaps most interesting of all is Lefler's concluding chapter, in which he compares and contrasts Aelred's and Thomas's writings

16. Ibid., xii.

17. Nathan Lefler, *Theologizing Friendship: How Amicitia in the Thought of Aelred and Aquinas Inscribes the Scholastic Turn* (Eugene, OR: Pickwick Publications, 2014).

18. I cannot do Aelred's beautiful and sublime insights justice here. To whet readers' appetites I will simply note that, building upon St. Augustine's exegesis of the book of Genesis, Aelred explains that God's rest on the Sabbath is indeed charity itself, that the mutual delight and Divine Charity of the Father and the Son is substantial and constitutes the Holy Spirit, that the easy yoke and light burden Christ refers to are the yoke and burdens of charity, and that the "three Sabbaths" of the seventh day of the week, the seventh year, and the jubilee of fiftieth year (the year following a Sabbath of Sabbath years) correspond to the three principal objects of charity—self, neighbor, and God.

on friendship in both content and style, using categories of Christological or transcendent, Johannine or Aristotelian, dramatic or scientific, friendly versus useful exegesis, biblical versus non-biblical, beautiful versus clear, erotic versus scientifically neutral, personal versus impersonal, and persuasive versus demonstrative. He argues that the first word in each pairing most aptly describes the approach of Aelred and the second that of Aquinas. Perhaps readers familiar only with the summaries and samples I have provided will have a sense of where Lefler is coming from.

I should note that, in classifying Thomas's writings on friendship as "non-biblical," Lefler does not declare that Thomas's writings contradict the Bible, but that Aelred's are more in keeping with the exegetical traditions of the Church Fathers and monastics. His writings on spiritual friendship grew out of monastic life, grounded in the *lectio divina* of meditative scriptural reading, while Thomas's are clearly grounded in the philosophy of Aristotle and are apt to employ scriptural references in the *ad hoc* manner of proof texts, clarifying and providing scriptural authority for points first made through logical argumentation. In Aquinas's writings on friendship we find the relatively impersonal voice of reason; though in every article of every question we find a first person "I" in the "*I answer that...*" section, Thomas tells us little of himself, let alone of his personal friendships. By contrast, Aelred could hardly be more personal, personable, and revealing in demonstrating friendship within his own life.

In their respective legacies, Aelred and Thomas reveal the heart and the mind of friendship: spiritual friendships that begin on earth and endure into heaven, loving God with the love of charity for His own sake, and our neighbors as ourselves, grounded in proper self-love, and raised to the heights of perfection by He who dwells with us in friendship whenever two or more friends are gathered in His name.

Conclusion:
Fostering and Enjoying
Genuine Friendships Today

You are not surprised at the number of students who choose to write their short paper on Aristotle on friendship. You smile. You wrote on the same topic too about their age and later when you were supposed to be more mature. Friendship is the greatest of all human topics, even reaching to the divinity.

~Fr. James V. Schall, S.J., *Docilitas*[1]

A faithful friend is a sturdy shelter; he that has found one has found a treasure.

~Sirach 6:14

ALAS, FR. SCHALL, I had no opportunity to write a short paper on Aristotle on friendship during my college years, yet here, too, am I, thirty-odd years later and supposedly more mature, writing a short book on friendship, Aristotle and all. The topic of friendship is truly great, and we have seen that two of the greatest of all thinkers in the time before Christ crafted timeless works on the subject. That friendship reaches to the divinity has been made clear as well, as we have seen how two of the holiest thinkers after the time of Christ have crafted their own timeless works on friendship, wherein the Divine is its source and summit. If you have a faithful friend, you surely don't need me (or perhaps even Joshua ben Sira) to tell you what a treasure you possess. In fact, I would hope that all of this reading about friendship has inspired my readers to form and to

---

1. James V. Schall, S.J., *Docilitas: On Teaching and Being Taught* (South Bend, IN: St. Augustine's Press, 2016), 5.

foster treasured friendships of their own, with others, with themselves, and with He through whom we all live, breathe, and have our being.

To conclude, I will provide some closing thoughts on our four "friends" of centuries past. I will also suggest to readers some modern "friends" who have encountered one or more of our four friends and whose insights might likewise help us to treasure our friendships and to suffuse them with the divine. Finally, I'll finish with a few reflections on how we might grow virtuous, harmonious, spiritual, and charitable friendships, perhaps even from the imperfect soils of the friendships of pleasure or utility—those carnal or worldly relationships that sometimes are mistaken for true friendships.

The Fantastic Four Evangelists of Friendship

As Matthew, Mark, Luke, and John have crafted the gospels proclaiming the good news of Christ, so, too, have Aristotle, Cicero, Aelred, and Thomas crafted four of the greatest works on the good news of friendship, the latter two basing their writings upon the words of Christ Himself, He who enabled us to become friends of God. Because Aristotle and Cicero lived before Christ, a more apt designation than *evangelists of friendship* would be that of *prophets of friendship*, for it seems fitting to propose that, as Christ told us he came not to abolish the Law and the Prophets, but to fulfill them (Matt. 5:17), so, too, did he not abolish the noble writings produced by the philosophers, but fulfill them, giving them the fullness of life, even unto eternal life.

Christ, like Aristotle and Cicero before him, calls us to lives of virtue. Indeed, he surpasses them in his call: "You, therefore, must be perfect, as your heavenly Father is perfect" (Matt. 5:48). He acknowledges that living up to the God-given potentials within us is no easy thing; indeed, to rise to the standard Christ's cross raised for us, we must deny ourselves and take up his cross in order to follow him (Matt. 16:24). Yet Christ also tells us that his yoke is easy and his burden light (Matt. 11:30). St. Aelred expounded on Christ's yoke as follows:

Yes, his yoke is easy and his burden light: therefore you will find rest for your souls. This yoke does not oppress, but unites; this burden has wings, not weight. This yoke is charity. This burden is brotherly love.[2]

The intellect of St. Thomas Aquinas, the "Angelic Doctor," took to flight with those same wings of charity to show just how close and how far that "burden" of charity extends—within, to ourselves, and indeed, to our own bodies, and outward and upward to God and neighbor in the holy bonds of true friendship forged by charity.

What Shall We Read to Grow Loving Friendships?

Readers are, of course, directed to the writings of the four evangelists of friendship, both the works summarized here and other relevant texts: the seventh book of Aristotle's *Eudemian Ethics*, which appears to be an earlier exposition of friendship; Cicero's *On Duties*, in which he expounds on the kinds of virtues that would make virtuous friendships possible; Aelred's masterwork *The Mirror of Charity*, a spiritual classic that provides a rich theological grounding for his later *Spiritual Friendship*; and St. Thomas's other writings on friendship scattered throughout his works, including his *Commentary of the Gospel of St. John*, in which he elaborates on John 15, the scene of the Last Supper in which Christ told his disciples that they were his friends and commanded them to love one another.

Here I will recommend a few recent writings on friendship that incorporate the traditions of at least two or three of our "four friendships," and which should be of special interest to Catholics or to anyone open to learning modern Catholic thinking on the nature and the experience of friendship:

Father Philip Halfacre's *Genuine Friendship: The Foundation for All Personal Relationships, Including Marriage and the Relationship with God* (Midwest Theological Forum) nicely addresses what its

---

2. Aelred of Rievaulx, *The Mirror of Charity*, Elizabeth Connor, trans. (Kalamazoo, MI: Cistercian Publications, 1990), 133.

subtitle proclaims, includes a brief look at Aristotle's, Cicero's, and Aelred's writings on friendship, and is rich in the wisdom of modern Christian thinkers, including Josef Pieper, C. S. Lewis, and Pope St. John Paul II.

Mary DeTurris Poust's *Walking Together: Discovering the Catholic Tradition of Spiritual Friendship* provides a much-needed and insightful female perspective on friendship. She incorporates the wisdom of Aelred's *Spiritual Friendship* and was inspired in part by St. Frances de Sales (1567–1622), best known for his masterpiece *Introduction to the Devout Life,* and also famous for his friendship and extensive correspondence with St. Jane Frances de Chantal (1572–1641), for whom he served as spiritual director. Poust covers the often-neglected topic of spiritual friendships between men and women, and highlights another noteworthy male-female friendship in the annals of Christianity: that of Blessed Jordan of Saxony (1190–1237), St. Dominic's successor as head of the Dominican Order, and the Dominican nun Blessed Diana d'Andalo (1201–1236). Many of Jordan's beautiful letters to Diana are preserved in Gerald Vann's *To Heaven with Diana!* (iUniverse, 2006).

An accessible and thoughtful summary of virtue and friendship, grounded in Aristotle and raised up through later Christian thought, may be found in Professor John Cuddeback's *True Friendship: Where Virtue Becomes Happiness* (Denver, CO: Epic Publishing, 2010), which I have also enjoyed in an audio version through the Catholic Courses programs of TAN Books/St. Benedict Press. I believe that both the book and the audio or video course are exceptionally well-suited as introductions, for students or adults, to the world of virtuous or "true" friendship.

The most recent contribution I have come across is Fr. Gary Lauenstein, C.Ss.R.'s *The Heart of Holiness: Friendship with God and Others,* (San Francisco: Ignatius, 2016). Father Lauenstein cites the three A's (Aristotle, Aelred, and Aquinas) as well as a host of other authors on the topic of friendship, including St. Alphonsus Ligouri (1696–1786), Doctor of the Church and founder of the Redemptorist Order, of which he is a member. The subtitle does not tell the whole story, however, for the book also includes an insightful chapter on "Friendship with Ourselves."

There is also a modern Catholic literature specifically focusing on what it means to share friendship with Christ, and several of these books have made it to my desk (and easy chair).

First published in 1912 and based on a series of sermons from 1910 and 1911, Msgr. Robert Hugh Benson's *The Friendship of Christ* (Veritas Splendor Publications, 2012) presents a broad overview of friendship with Christ in terms of the interior life in pursuit of spiritual perfection, of the exterior relationship with Christ's Church, and through examination of the words and acts of Christ crucified.

Gary Zimak's recent book *Find a Real Friend in Jesus: Ten Amazingly Easy Steps* (Servant Books, 2016) provides a decidedly intimate and Catholic approach to forming a personal relationship with Jesus Christ. As the subtitle declares, Zimak provides a step-by-step program whereby we may truly discover Christ as our "best best friend" and let our hearts rest and find joy in Him.

Ascending the Ladder to Divine Friendship with the Help of Our Four Friends

I will close first with a practical, down-to-earth suggestion and secondly with a more heavenly reflection.

Hopefully the works of these four saints have given us some grist for the mills of our minds as we examine the friendships within our own lives. Are Tom, Dick, and Harry, or Sue, Jill, and Sherry our true friends in virtue and charity? Are we concerned with the pleasure that they provide or the benefits they bring us, rather than cherishing each of them for their own sakes as our second selves? Do we participate in conversations and activities that reflect our love for what is highest and noblest in ourselves as we spur one another to a happiness born of the joint pursuit of virtue? As we share in the activities of our lives, do we ever reflect upon the fact that when we are gathered together, Christ dwells among us? If our friendships, upon reflection, seem to bear out the Philosopher's observation that true friendships of virtue are rare, what might we do to remedy the relationships that fall short of that bill?[3]

Philosopher Gregory Sadler makes an interesting suggestion in

---

3. Not to mention our relationships with Facebook "friends," which bear little

his aforementioned article, "How Hard is it to Find an Aristotelian Friend?," suggesting that we should not hold fast to Aristotle's three kinds of friendship as rigid categories, but should look upon them as a continuum. Reflecting upon his own relationships, Dr. Sadler notes that friendships built upon pleasure or usefulness may develop into true friendships of virtue, as time spent in pleasant or useful interactions with others may expose us to good qualities of their characters and draw us toward a deeper appreciation of the nobler elements at the core of their personalities. He posits that true friendships are not rare things reserved for sages or saints, but are readily available to those on the road to virtue.

Aelred might well have agreed with this optimistic view regarding the potential for friendships of virtue that start on less firm relational ground. While we are to extend the love of charity even to our enemies, as Thomas spelled out with such precision, Aelred notes that when we follow Christ's command to "love your enemies and do good to those who hate you" (cf. Matt. 5:44–45), we may free those who are "slaves to sin" (cf. Matt. 6:12), helping them to become "not only a freeman but even a friend."[4]

Let us, then, be on the alert for potential virtuous and spiritual friends, not only from the ranks of our friends of pleasure or utility, but perhaps even among those who are now our enemies. Such transformation is made possible through friendship in Christ, a friendship that will continue eternally in heaven with God and with the entire Communion of Saints.

Some have complained that heaven might get boring, what with the eternal strumming of harps and so forth, but just imagine the unlimited opportunities to enjoy eternal friendships with humans, angels, and God. I, for one, would love to eavesdrop on the conversation between four great friends across time, as the philosopher, the statesman, the abbot, and the professor converse and grow in their friendship, joined by the carpenter who came to call them, and all of us, friends.

---

relation to ancient conceptions of *philia* and *amicitia* that presumed some amount of in-person interaction!

4. Aelred of Rievaulx, *Mirror of Charity*, 229 (III, 4,10).

About the Author

Kevin Vost (b. 1961) holds a Psy.D. in Clinical Psychology from Adler University in Chicago. He has taught at Aquinas College in Nashville, the University of Illinois at Springfield, MacMurray College, and Lincoln Land Community College. He has served as a research review committee member for American Mensa, a society promoting the scientific study of human intelligence, and as an advisory board member for the International Association of Resistance Trainers, an organization that certifies personal fitness trainers.

Dr. Vost is the author of over a dozen Catholic books, has appeared on hundreds of Catholic radio and television broadcasts, and has traveled across the United States and Ireland, giving talks on the themes of his books. When home, he drinks great draughts of coffee while studying timeless Thomistic tomes in the company of his wife, their two sons, and their two dogs in Springfield, Illinois.